FLEXUS

TRUMPET CALISTHENICS FOR THE MODERN IMPROVISOR

LAURIE FRINK & JOHN MCNEIL

Flexus

Laurie Frink & John McNeil

OmniTonePress
500 2nd Street Suite 2
Brooklyn, New York 11215-2503
www.OmniTonePress.com
flexus@OmniTonePress.com

Cover Design: Frank Tafuri
Interior Design: Andrew Green

ISBN 0-9748544-0-9

Thanks to:

Lois Martin
Lolly Bienenfeld
Carmine Caruso
Andrew Green
Jeni Taylor
Dan Steinhilber
J.C. Sanford
Sarah Wilson
Mike Walters
Frank Tafuri

About the Authors

Laurie Frink

Laurie Frink has been a freelance trumpet player in New York City since the 1970's. In addition to extensive recording work, she has played trumpet with Benny Goodman, Gerry Mulligan, Mel Lewis, Maria Schneider, Andrew Hill, Dave Liebman and Kenny Wheeler. She is a member of the faculties of New York University, The New School and the Manhattan School of Music.

John McNeil

John McNeil is a jazz trumpet player living in Brooklyn, New York. He has played with Horace Silver, Gerry Mulligan, The Thad Jones/Mel Lewis Orchestra and many others. John has led his own groups since the late 1970's and has recorded many critically acclaimed CD's. He is also an active writer/producer on the New York Jazz scene.

CONTENTS

INTRODUCTION 6

FLEXUS 7

PRACTICING 8

HOW TO USE THIS BOOK 10

PRELIMINARY STUDIES: Long Setting 12

FLEXIBILITY 18

ONE • BASIC FLEXIBILITIES 18
TWO • FLEXANDO 24
THREE • ADVANCED FLEXIBILITIES 28
FOUR • INTERVAL STUDIES 44
ETUDE ONE 49
ETUDE TWO 50
ETUDE THREE 52

ARTICULATION 54

ONE • SLURRING/TONGUING 54
ETUDE FOUR 59
TWO • DEVELOPED SCALE 60
THREE • ARPEGGIOS/DIRECTION CHANGES 74
ETUDE FIVE 82

PEDAL TONES 84

QUICK REGISTER CHANGES 90

ONE • CONSISTENT INTERVALS 90
TWO • SPIDERS 98
ETUDE SIX 104
THREE • CHROMATIC DISPLACEMENT 106
FOUR • TARGET PRACTICE 118
FIVE • OCTAVE DISPLACEMENT 122
ETUDE SEVEN 126
ETUDE EIGHT 130
ETUDE NINE 132
ETUDE TEN 134

CD CONTENTS 135

INTRODUCTION

As an improvising trumpet player, you face unique physical challenges:

- You are more often than not operating at the limits of your technical ability.
- The mouthpiece is on the lips for long periods of time, creating endurance problems.
- Emotion can take over, making you play louder and with more intensity.
- In an improvised solo there is often a dizzying array of articulations, dynamics, register changes and tone variations.

All of these conditions are difficult to duplicate when practicing.

In preparing a written piece, even a very difficult one, your body learns to accomplish the consecutive muscular demands of the piece through repetition. The improvising musician doesn't have this luxury. By definition, improvisation is spontaneous and unrehearsed. Such unrehearsed, unplanned movements can leave the body scrambling to coordinate itself, which invites extraneous motion and can exacerbate existing bad habits.

It's a fact that the content of your improvisation is determined in large part by your technique. You tend not to conceive ideas that are physically beyond you. Therefore, to expand your vocabulary, you must improve your instrumental skill.

Although you can't practice inspiration, you can prepare your body to execute what you are inspired to play. Therefore, to improvise music with a wide variety of elements, you have to practice a wide variety of techniques. As in all things musical, consistent practice is necessary for consistent performance.

FLEXUS contains a wide range of technique- and endurance-building exercises that address all of the fundamental elements necessary to play the trumpet freely and easily. It is designed to help improvisors in all musical idioms—jazz, classical and any others. FLEXUS synthesizes the teaching techniques of Laurie Frink, John McNeil and Carmine Caruso, and represents an evolution in trumpet practice that combines time-honored exercises with new and unique concepts to create a technical approach for the 21st century.

FLEXUS

To improvise effectively, the physical act of playing needs to be a conditioned reflex—freedom of expression is only possible when the physical demands of playing are under control. To this end, FLEXUS asks the student to momentarily put aside the study of music itself and instead practice the muscular movements involved in playing the instrument.

Learning comes through exposure and repetition—you expose yourself to what you want to learn and then repeat the exposure. The great brass teacher Carmine Caruso used the analogy of a baby learning to walk; the baby experiences nothing but failure in its attempts until the first successful step. It does not judge itself for its failures, but simply tries again. It is the repetition of an action *with no judgement attached* that achieves the desired result. No schedule or time frame is necessary. With enough repetition, any movement becomes a conditioned reflex.

Timing and coordination are 100% of trumpet playing. What we call coordination is just the synchronized movement of muscles *in time*. When given a consistent tempo, muscles coordinate much more easily. This results in muscular balance, which leads to greater facility and endurance. To put it another way, a balanced embouchure functions effortlessly and allows you to move freely and easily, whereas muscles that are out of balance work harder than they need to and thus get tired faster. Playing or practicing with inconsistent time also greatly reduces your accuracy—it's like trying to hit a moving target while you yourself are moving.

It is also of utmost importance to feed a steady stream of air to the lips. No matter what the physical demands—wide leaps, accents, quick movements, etc.—the air stream needs to be consistent and constantly moving to maintain good intonation and flexibility. If you don't concentrate enough on keeping steady air, the muscular movements of the embouchure and tongue can interrupt the air stream, resulting in an unfocused sound and inconsistent performance.

When undertaking a new course of study, the temptation is to abandon one's existing trumpet routine. We advise instead that new exercises be worked into a practice routine over a period of several weeks. Through performing the right exercises daily, poor habits will gradually be replaced as the muscles naturally find their most efficient balance.

PRACTICING

The studies in FLEXUS should be viewed as calisthenics and played with abandon. Because the demands are muscular rather than musical, no musical value judgements need apply. Even the etudes, though compositional in nature, should be approached as physical skill builders.

This book will often push you to the limit of your abilities or beyond. As a result, tone quality may suffer while exercises are being performed. Don't let the sound or feel of an exercise affect how it is practiced.

The Right Message

To practice efficiently, it is necessary to maintain a consistent approach and insist that the body conform to it. It's better to practice at a very slow tempo that permits playing everything in time than to attempt a faster tempo that necessitates slowing down for difficult passages. To intermittently slow down sends the message that slowing down is acceptable and that it's not necessary to acquire the skill to perform the passage in time. Conversely, if a steady tempo is maintained, the body and the subconscious are given the message that slowing down is not permitted and they need to acquire the necessary skills to perform the passage at that tempo.

Similarly, Long Setting exercises (see page 12), by not allowing multiple readjustments, give the message that the entire range of the trumpet can be played with a single embouchure set.

Timing and Subdivision

Timing is the most basic element of trumpet playing, and to develop consistent timing, the *body* needs to be involved in the timekeeping process. For all exercises in this book, tap quarter notes with one foot and use the up/down motion to mark off upbeats and downbeats. Starting each exercise with four preparatory foot taps will help ensure secure attacks.

In addition to foot tapping, the focus of the conscious attention should be on mentally subdividing each beat into sixteenth notes to help guarantee steadiness of pulse. Subdivision narrows the window in which muscular movements can take place, and makes it more likely that the proper muscles will move together. This makes everything from wide leaps to lip trills easier to execute. Practicing studies while consciously subdividing eventually results in subdivision becoming a subconscious habit. Subdivision can even help with performance anxiety by taking the focus off of execution and putting it on timing.

Singing

Learn to sing any exercise that is difficult to hear or has complex motion. This is especially advisable with octave displacement exercises. Accurately singing an exercise dramatically increases the odds of playing it correctly. In addition, material that you can sing shows up in your improvisations more easily.

FLEXUS is meant to be used as a supplement to other kinds of practice. Many of the exercises in this book are physically strenuous and are designed for practice days, not performance days. Also, play these studies at or near the beginning of a practice session when the embouchure is fresh. *NEVER* play these exercises when fatigued. Practicing on a tired embouchure invites manipulation and forms bad habits very quickly.

HOW TO USE THIS BOOK

In a typical practice day, play at least one exercise from each section in the order presented, although the first exercises in one section can often be paired with the first exercises in other sections. Personal experience should help dictate the exact course followed in a given day.

Preliminary Studies

The exercises in this chapter are meant to be played in order. When Exercise One can be played comfortably, replace it with Exercise Two, then Exercise Three, etc. Only one of these exercises should be played in a single day.

Flexibility

Section One • Basic Flexibilities, pages 18 through 23
These exercises move quickly from one harmonic series to the next. Three or four daily.

Section Two • Flexando, pages 24 through 27
These exercises require a consistent, ever-moving air stream from low to high and vice versa. One or two daily.

Section Three • Advanced Flexibilities, pages 28 through 43
An assortment of more challenging flexibilities that require and develop a variety of skills. With the possible exception of the studies on pages 40 through 43, the exercises in this section should be attempted only after Sections One and Two can be played comfortably. Depending on your skill level, play several of these exercises daily.

Section Four • Interval Studies, pages 44 through 48
These exercises require slurring over consecutive fourths and fifths moving in the same direction. One or two daily.

Articulation

Section One • Slurring/Tonguing, pages 54 through 58
Maintaining the same tongue position whether slurring or tonguing over the entire harmonic series. Play every exercise in this section daily.

Section Two • Developed Scale, pages 60 through 70
Slurring and then tonguing scale fragments and/or diatonic intervals. These gradually lengthen and widen in scope, while the time in which they must be executed stays the same. Exercise Eleven is a different format, but is a useful compliment to Developed Scale exercises. Only one Developed Scale should be played in a single day, and can be combined with Exercise Eleven.

Section Three • Arpeggios/Direction Changes, pages 74 through 81
A series of arpeggiated chords which begin and end with a common tone. The exercises on page 81 teach repeated rapid change in direction. Depending on your skill level, play up to six a day.

Pedal Tones
Pages 84 through 89
In addition to the preparatory exercise on page 84, play only one other study from this section in a given day.

Quick Register Changes
Section One • Consistent Intervals, pages 90 through 97
Exercises that gradually accustom the embouchure to rapid changes in register through the use of consistent intervals. Three or four daily.

Section Two • Spiders, pages 98 through 103
Expanding interval exercises built around a central tone. One or two daily.

Section Three • Chromatic Displacement, pages 106 through 117
Descending chromatics within a standing pattern. Four or five daily.

Section Four • Target Practice, pages 118 through 121
Connecting the registers by playing the same three-note figure across four octaves. Three or four daily.

Section Five • Octave Displacement, pages 122 through 129
Displacement of one note, up or down, within a melodic line in both tonal and atonal exercises. These are the most challenging studies within Quick Register Changes. Your skill level will determine the number of exercises practiced.

THINGS TO REMEMBER:

- A balanced embouchure is the result of balanced practice. Therefore, don't play the exercises from any one chapter to the exclusion of other chapters.
- The instructions for one chapter don't necessarily apply to any other chapter.
- Because everyone learns at their own pace, the decision to move on to the next exercise has to be an individual one. It's not unusual to spend a couple of months on one exercise.
- When doing strenuous exercises, rest as much as you play.
- Long Setting is only to be used where indicated.

PRELIMINARY STUDIES

The preliminary studies on pages 13 through 17 are used to stabilize the embouchure and allow it to come into focus before adding motion or other challenges. They are adapted from Carmine Caruso's original six-note exercises.

These exercises are played without removing the mouthpiece from the lips and are referred to as "Long Setting" exercises. All breaths are taken through the nose, leaving the embouchure unbroken. These exercises teach the lips to move from one note to the next *inside* the mouthpiece, and to maintain the same setting throughout the full range of the instrument. Long setting practice reduces extraneous motion when moving between registers, and automatically increases endurance and accuracy.

By practicing this way, the body learns the relative position of each note. In Exercise One, whatever adjustments are made to get from G to C have to be undone to get back down to G on the repeat, thus making the notes feel closer together. Exercise Two extends this relationship to low C, and so on.

Note: Long setting exercises are not isometric. Mouthpiece pressure and tension in the corners should be relaxed during the measure rest.

Exercise One should be played once daily for approximately two weeks before replacing it with Variation I. Likewise, continue with Variation I for two weeks before replacing it with Variation II. When you replace Exercise One with Exercise Two, follow the same timetable before moving on to the variations. As stated on page 11, the number of weeks devoted to each exercise and its variations will vary with each individual. Move on only when you can play a study easily. One of these exercises should be a part of your daily routine as long as you continue to play the trumpet.

REMEMBER:

1. Use four preparatory foot taps to start each exercise.
2. Subdivide each beat into sixteenth notes.
3. Feed a steady stream of air to the lips.
4. Leave the mouthpiece on for the duration of the study.

H= Breath attack
T= Tongued attack
BTN= Breathe through the nose

One ♩ = 62–72

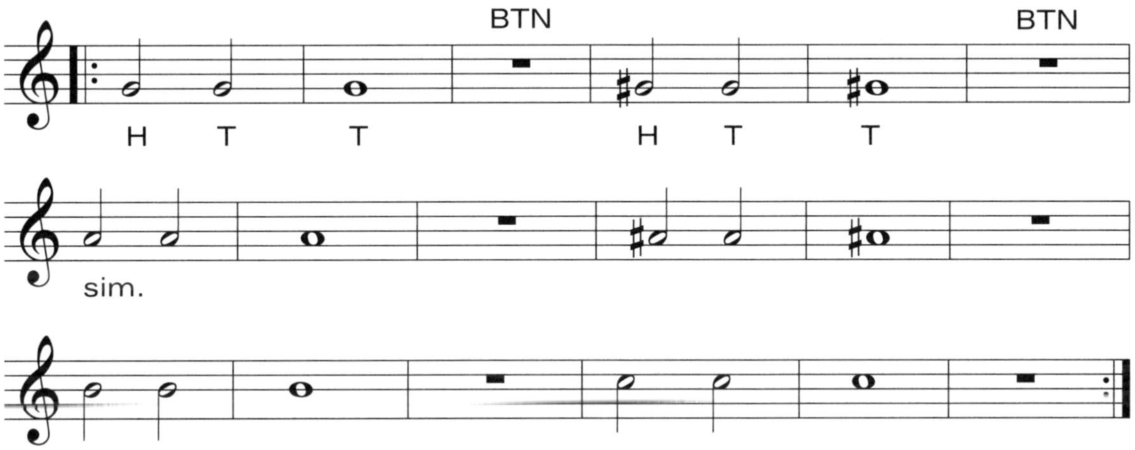

Apply the following variations to each pitch in the above exercise.

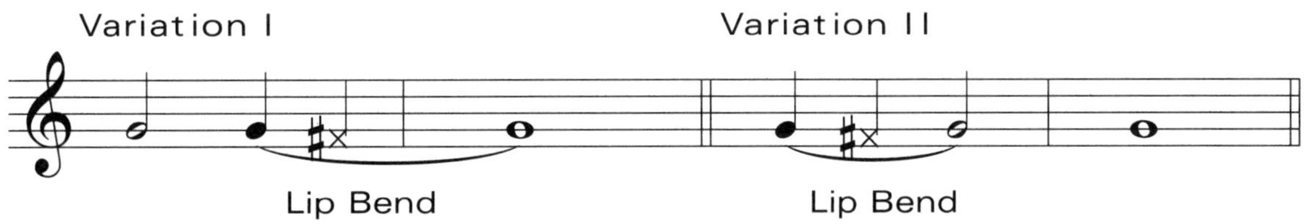

Lip Bends

A lip bend is achieved by using the lips instead of the valves to lower the pitch. The process of bending the pitch down and then returning enables the embouchure to find the resonant center of the pitch.

PRELIMINARY STUDIES

Two

Apply the following variations to each pitch in the above exercise.

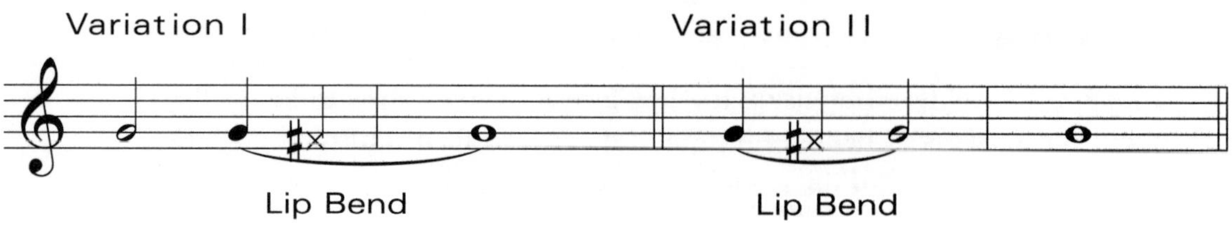

Three

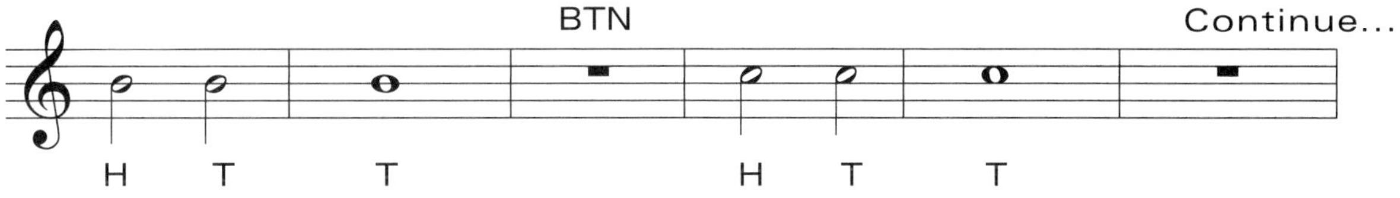

... applying the above pattern to the following pitches in order:

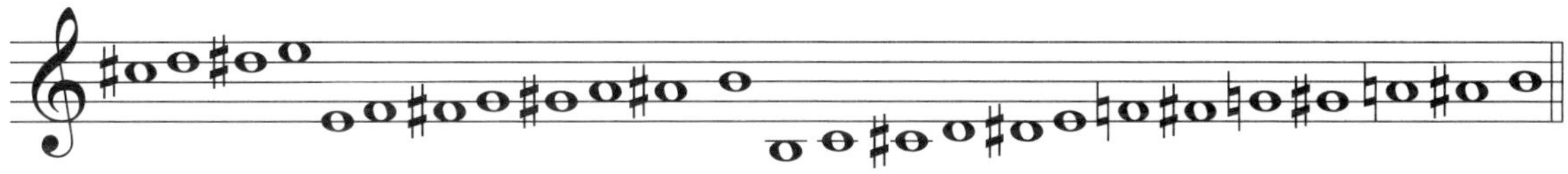

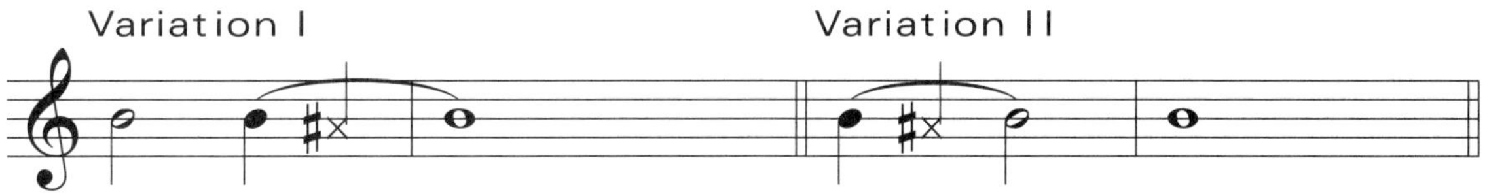

Four

... using all of the following pitches in order:

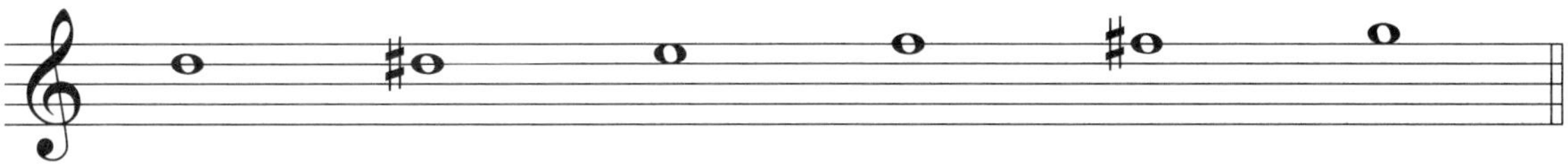

When comfortable with Exercise Four, add a repeat.

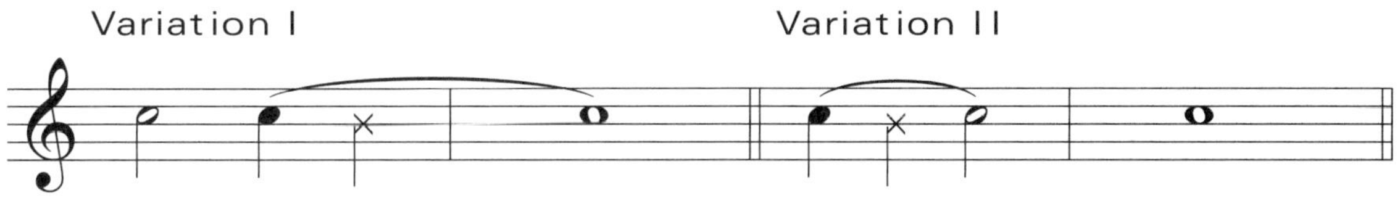

The pattern of breath and tongued attacks is the same through page 17. All breaths are through the nose.

PRELIMINARY STUDIES

Five

Continue...

... using all of the following pitches in order:

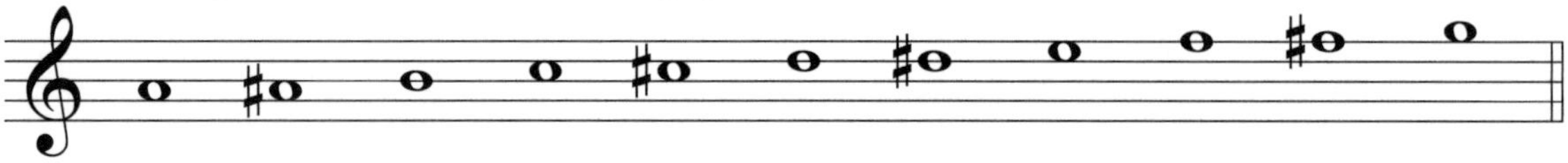

Variation I Variation II

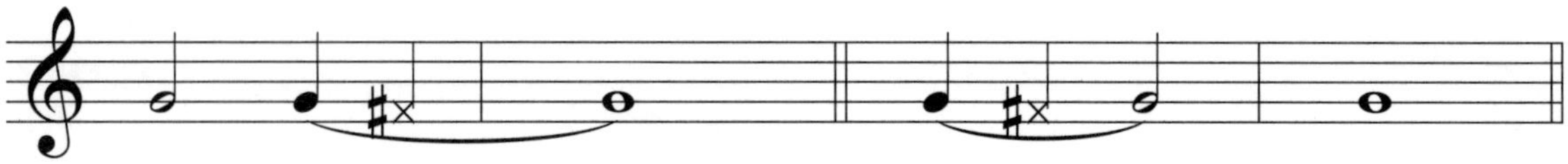

Six

Continue...

... using all of the following pitches in order:

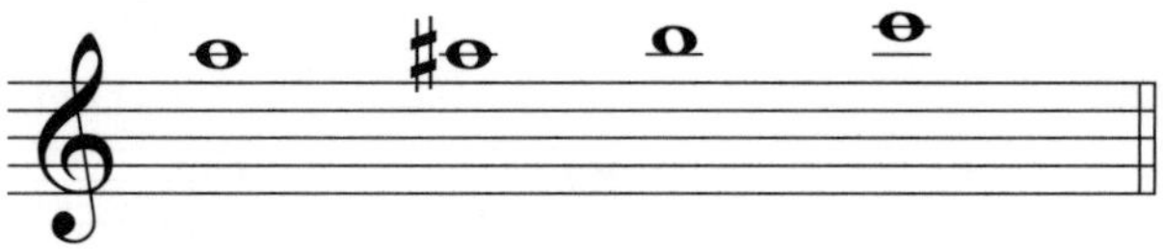

Variation I Variation II

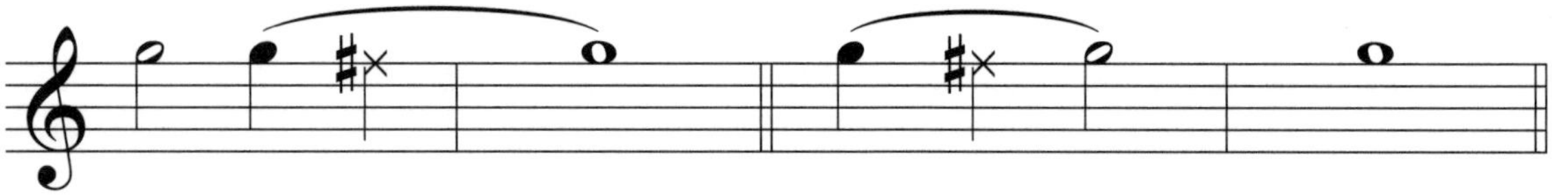

Seven

Continue...

... using all of the following pitches in order:

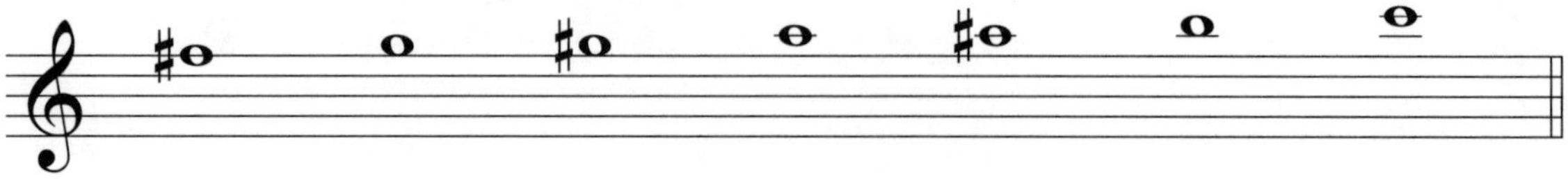

Variation I Variation II

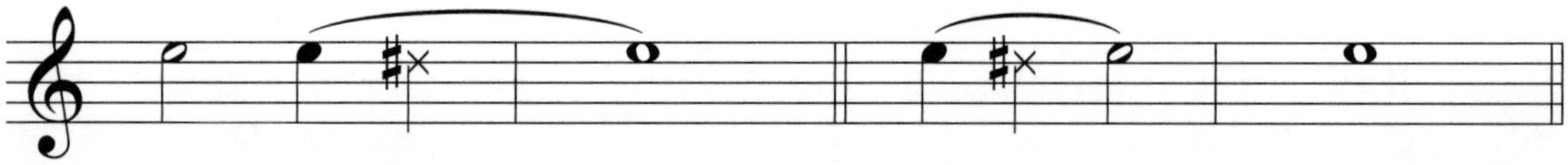

Eight

Continue...

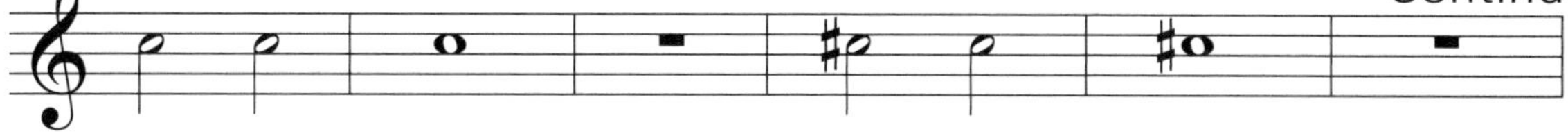

... using all of the following pitches in order:

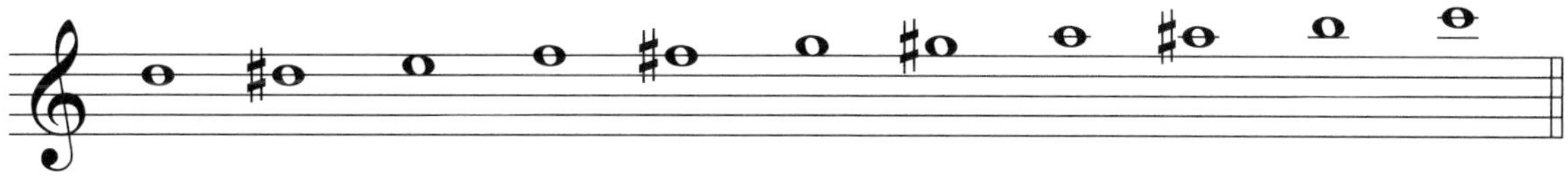

Variation I

Variation II

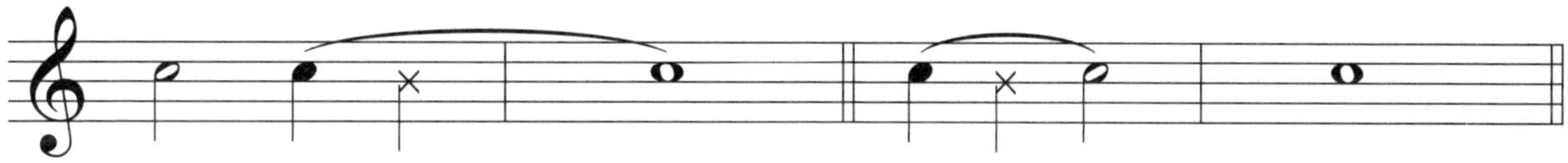

Nine

Continue...

... using all of the following pitches in order:

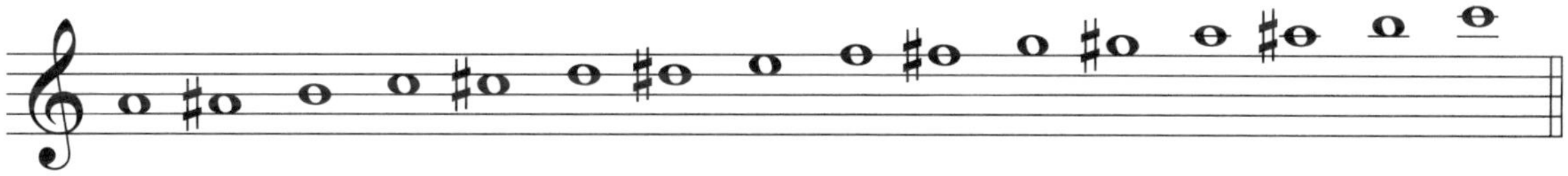

Variation I

Variation II

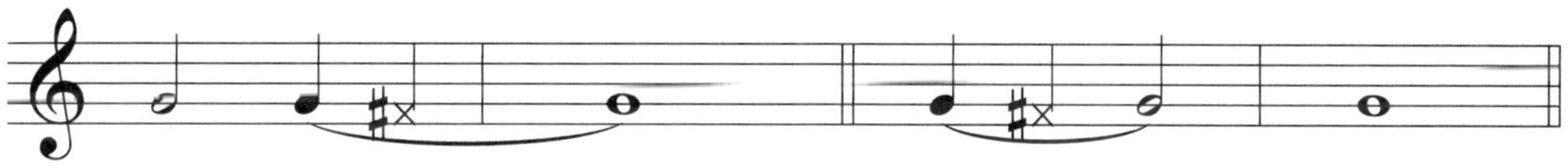

Ten

Continue...

... using all of the following pitches in order:

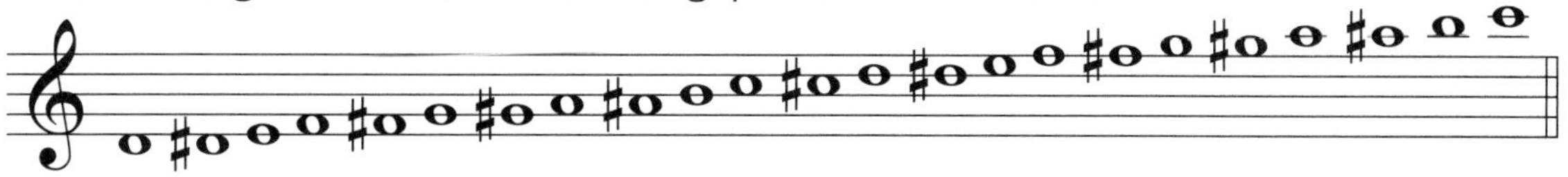

Variation I

Variation II

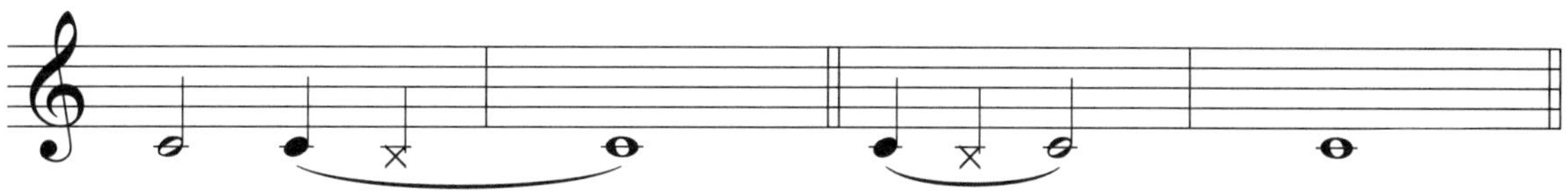

FLEXIBILITY

ONE • BASIC FLEXIBILITIES

Flexibility is the most fundamental trumpet skill. Maintaining a steady airstream is necessary for good flexibility, and flexibility studies in turn develop a consistent airstream.

The flexibility studies in this book begin at a fairly advanced level. If you have not worked out the basic mechanics of lip slurs and trills, you need to do so before attempting these exercises. Leave the mouthpiece on for the duration of each two-line segment.

One

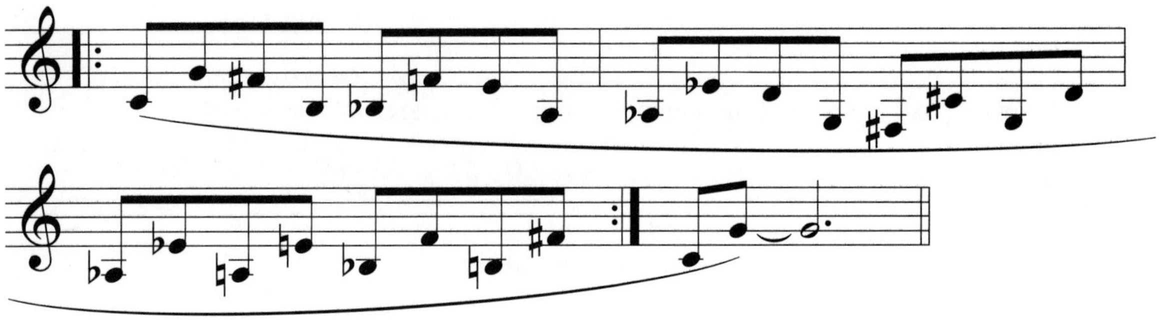

Two

Leave the mouthpiece on for the duration of each two-line segment

Three

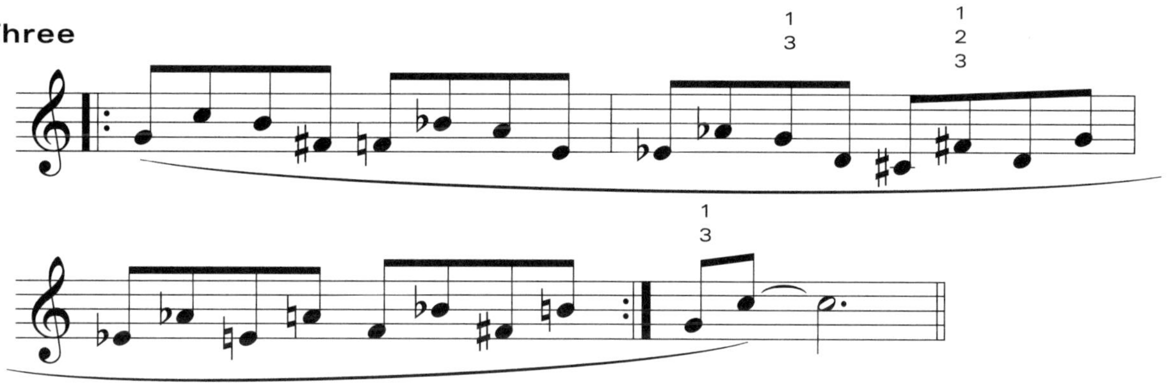

Four

Leave the mouthpiece on for the duration of each two-line segment

Five

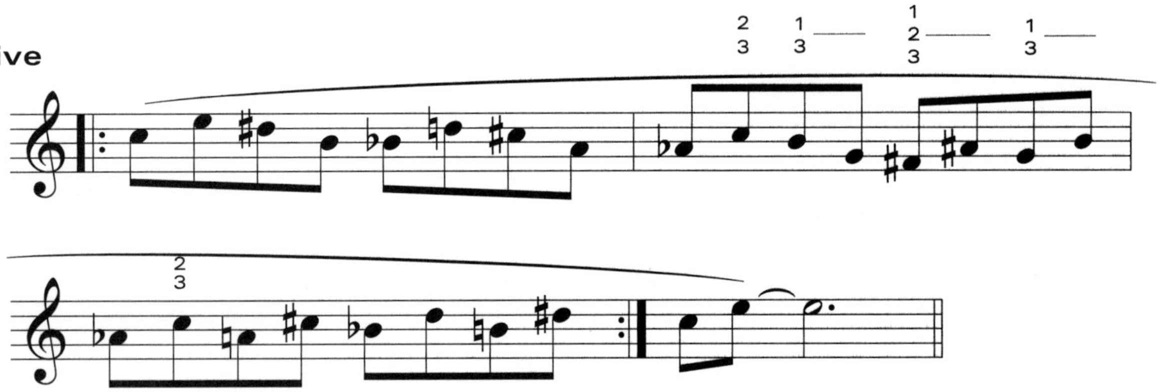

Six

Leave the mouthpiece on for the duration of each two-line segment.

Seven

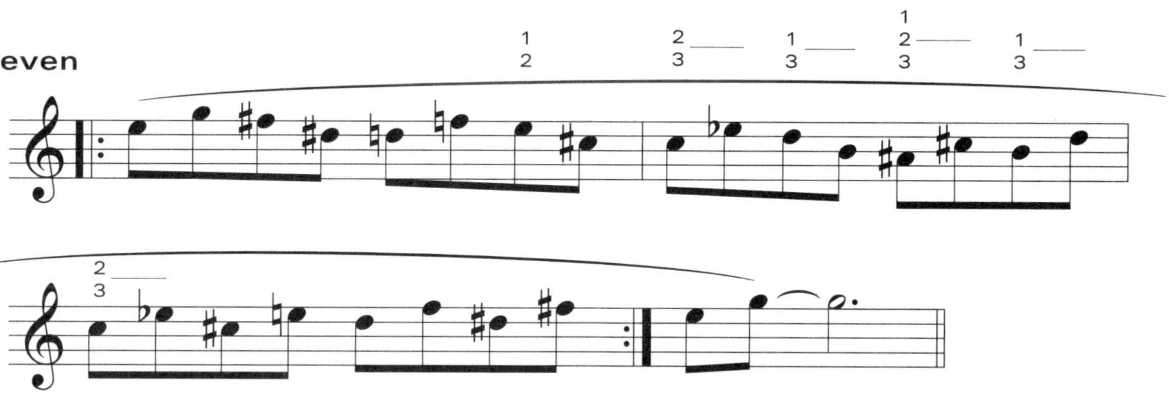

Eight

ONE • FLEXIBILITY

Leave the mouthpiece on for the duration of each two-line segment.

Nine

Ten

Leave the mouthpiece on for the duration of each two-line segment.

Eleven

TWO • FLEXIBILITY

TWO • FLEXANDO

The goal of these exercises is to maintain a continuous air stream from beginning to end—right through the change of direction. Aim for the final note to keep the air from stopping or faltering at the halfway point.

One

1

2

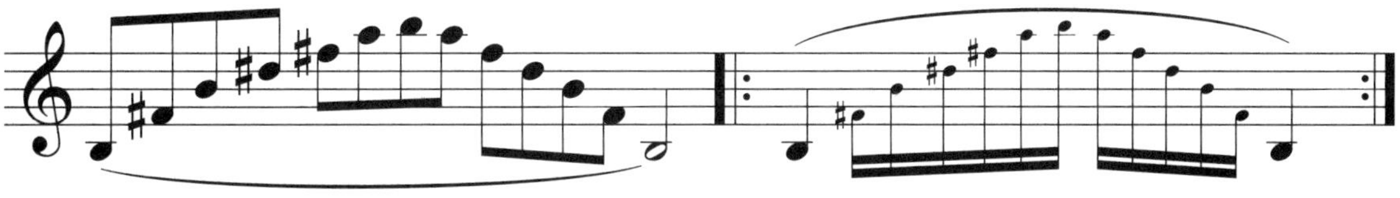

0

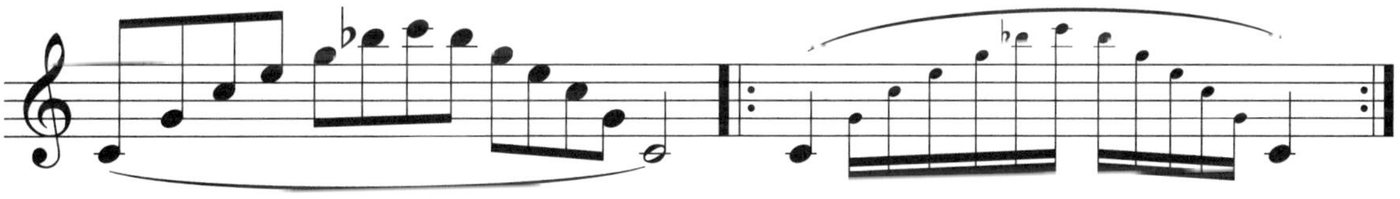

1
2
Two 3

Continue up the harmonic series as in Exercise One.

Three

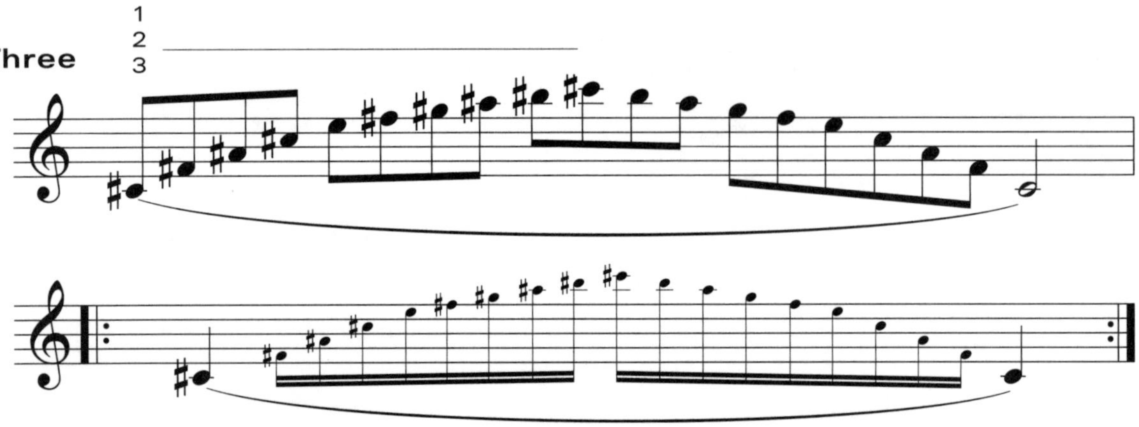

Continue up the harmonic series as in Exercise One.

Four

Continue up the harmonic series as in Exercise One.

Five

Continue up the harmonic series as in Exercise One.

1
2
3

Six

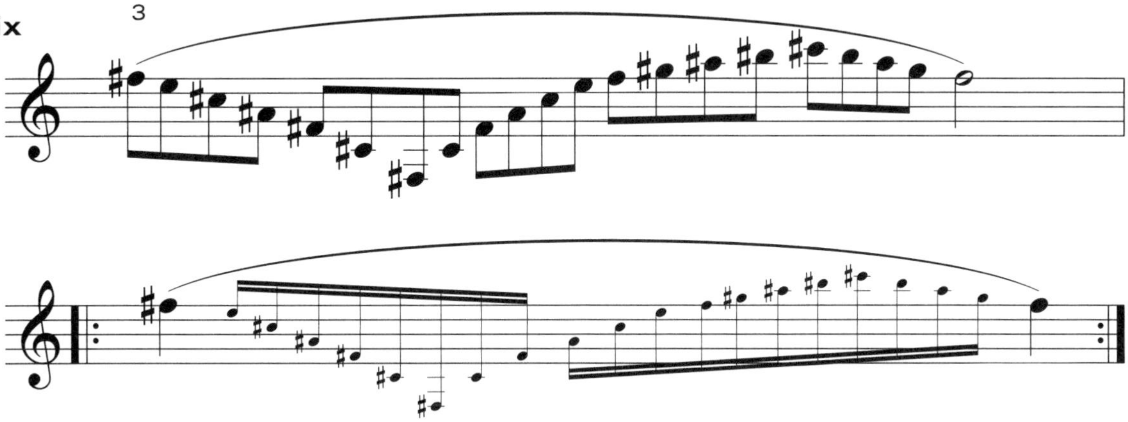

Continue up the harmonic series as in Exercise One.

1
2
3

Seven

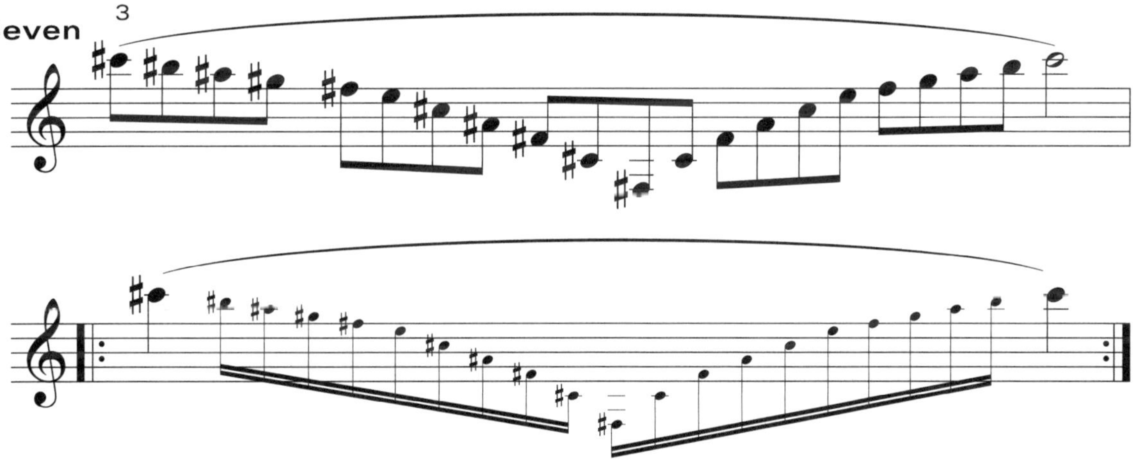

Continue up the harmonic series as in Exercise One.

THREE • ADVANCED FLEXIBILITIES

Reset after each line.

One

Reset after each line.

Two

THREE • FLEXIBILITY

Reset after each line.

Three

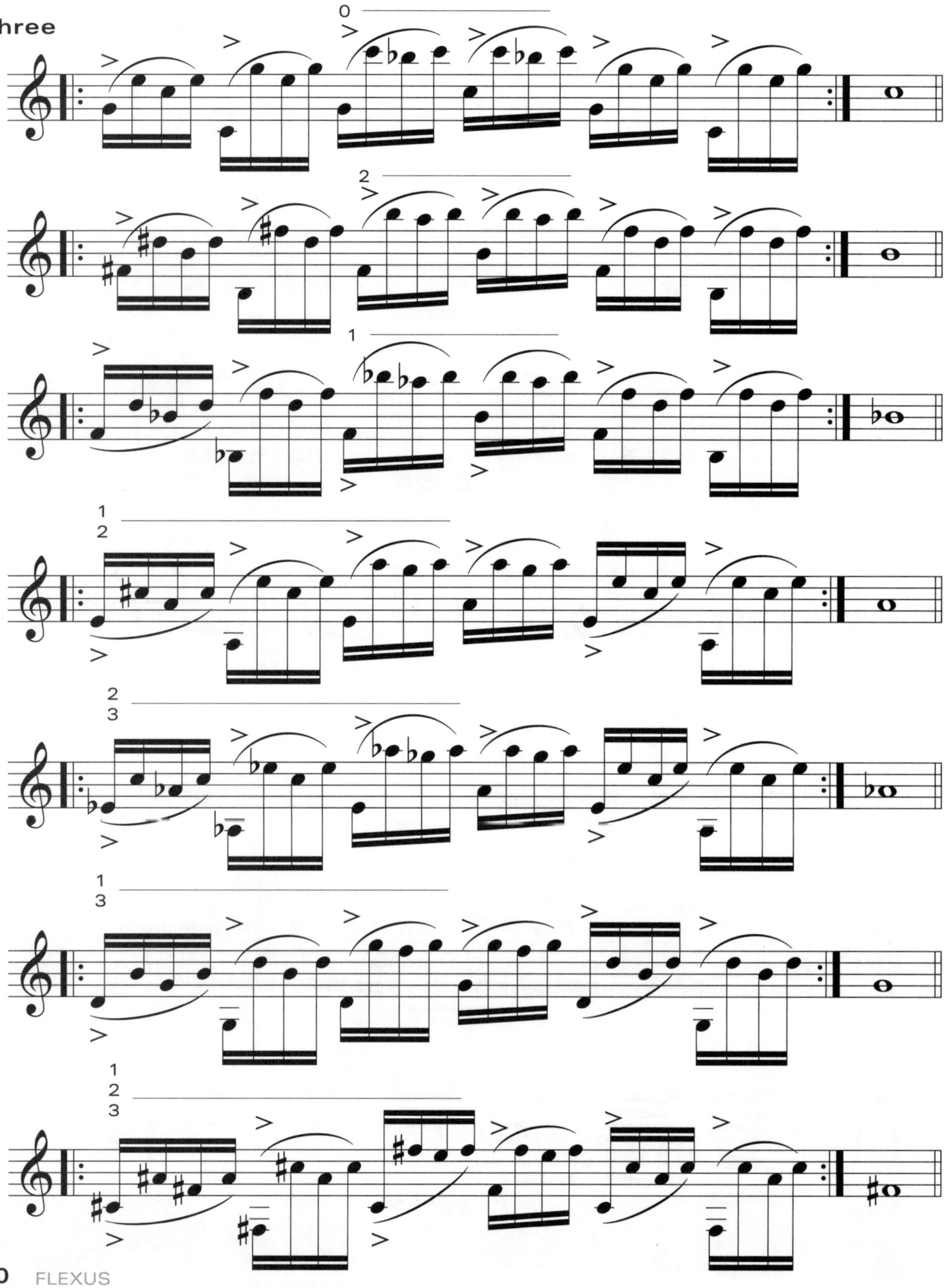

The following exercises are a continuation of those on pages 18 through 22.

Leave the mouthpiece on for the duration of each two-line segment.

One

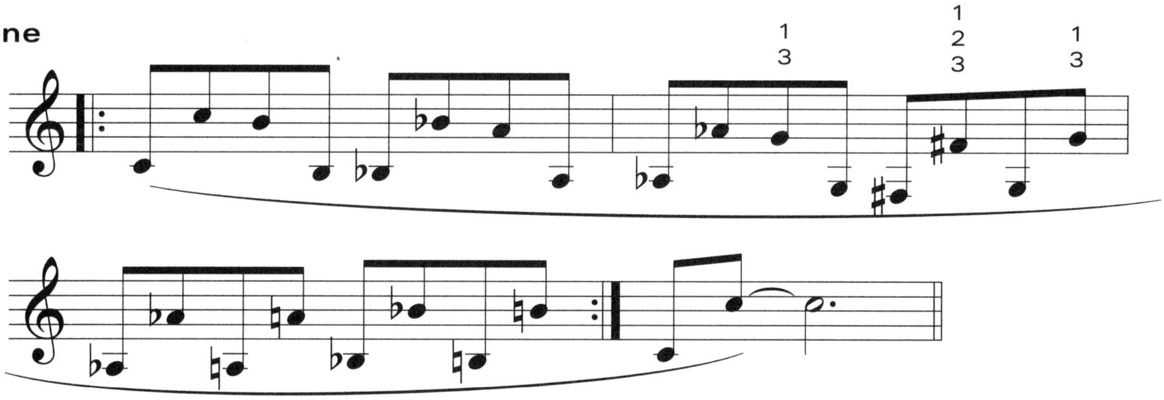

Two

THREE • FLEXIBILITY

Leave the mouthpiece on for the duration of each two-line segment.

Three

Four

Leave the mouthpiece on for the duration of each two-line segment.

Five

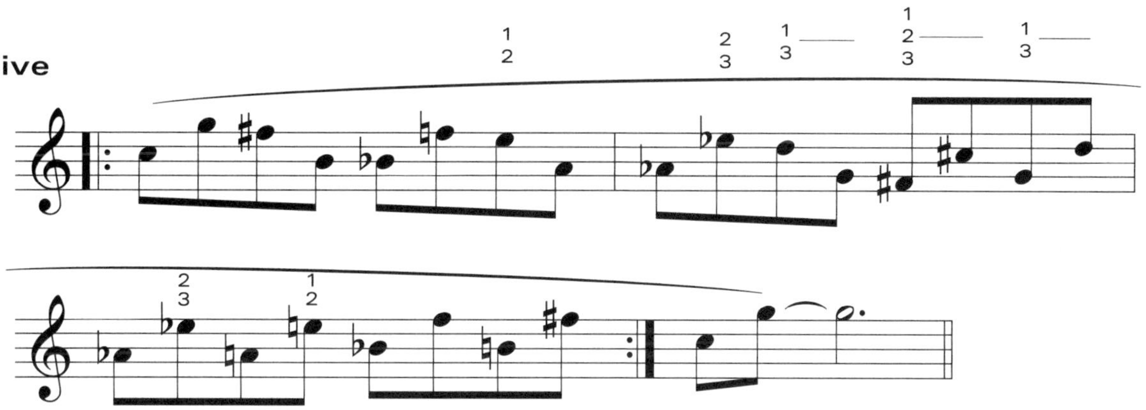

Six

Seven

THREE • FLEXIBILITY

Leave the mouthpiece on for the duration of each two-line segment.

Eight

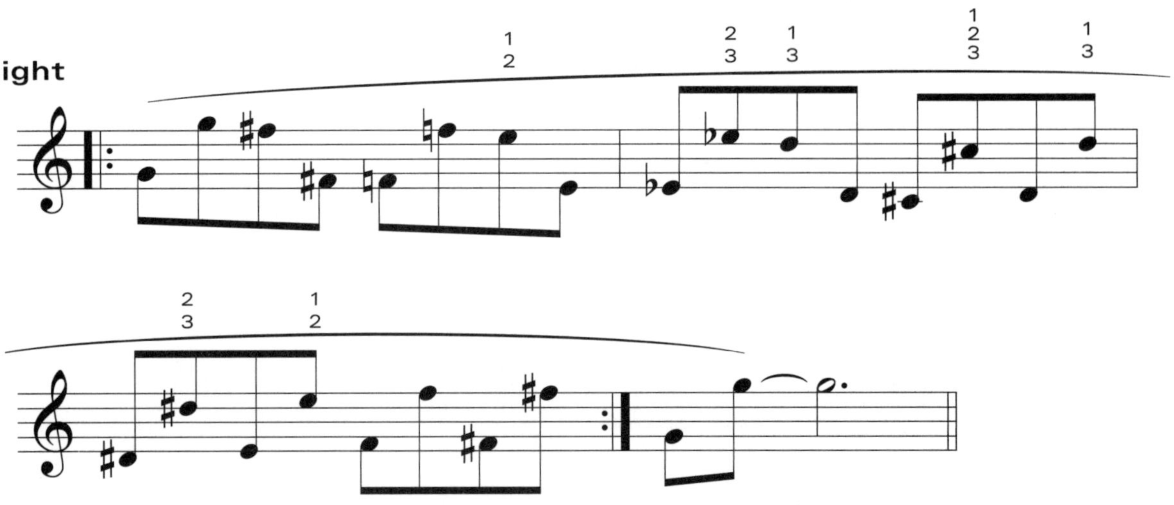

Nine

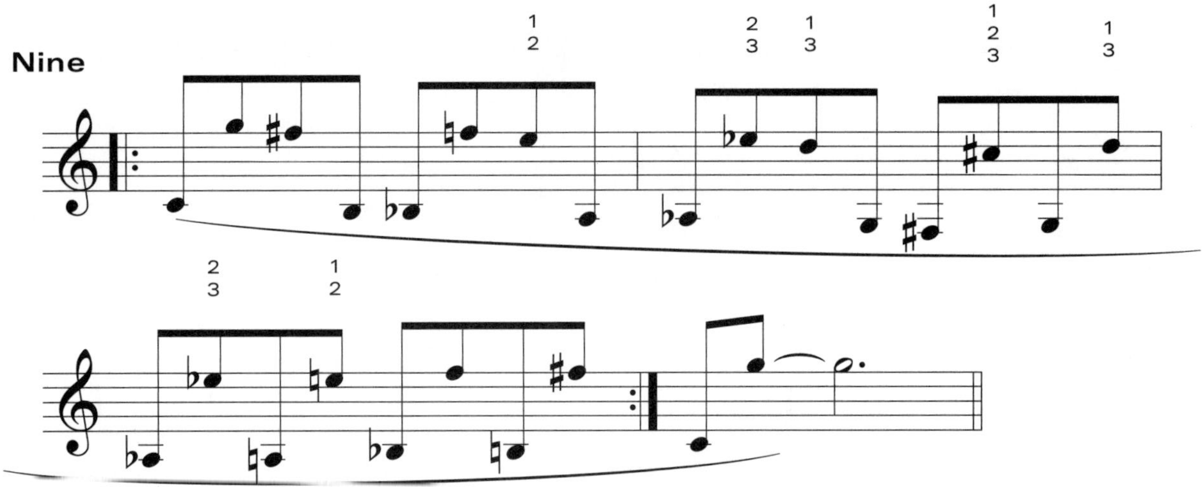

Ten

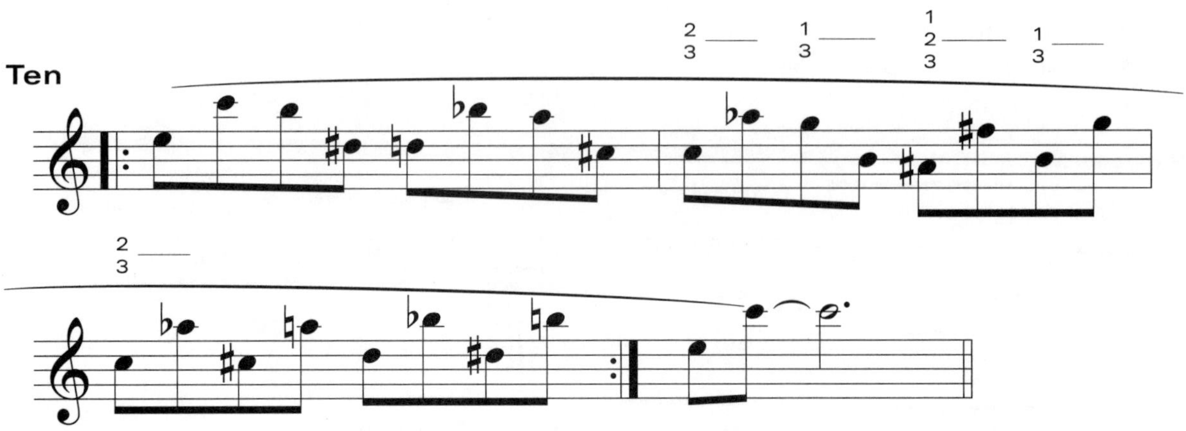

FLEXIBILITY • THREE

Leave the mouthpiece on for the duration of each two-line segment.

Eleven

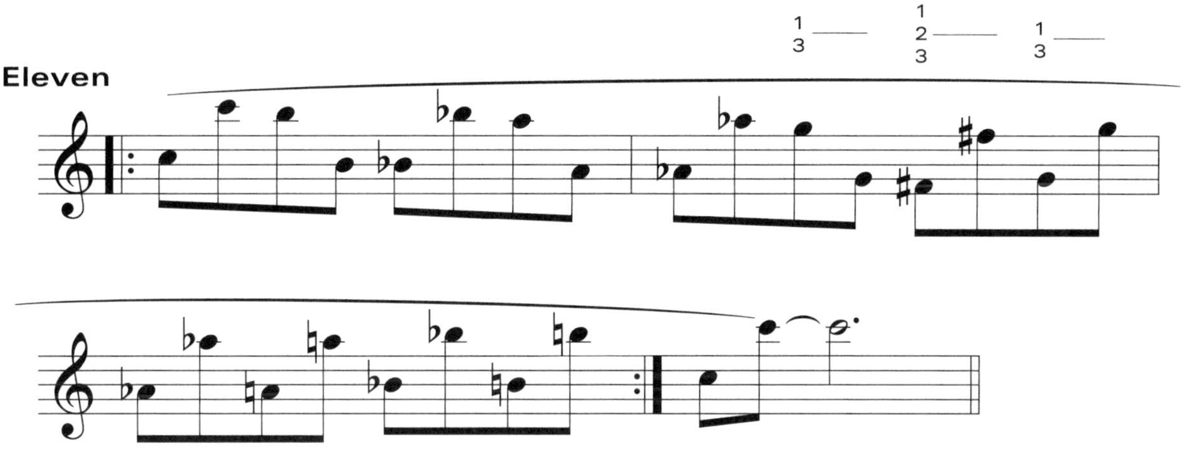

Twelve

Thirteen

THREE • FLEXIBILITY

One of the problems faced by brass players is maintaining flexibility at loud volumes. The following exercises address this problem. First, play an entire series softly. When this can be accomplished easily, add a very pronounced crescendo/decrescendo as marked. These exercises will teach the lips to remain focused and flexible at all volumes.

One

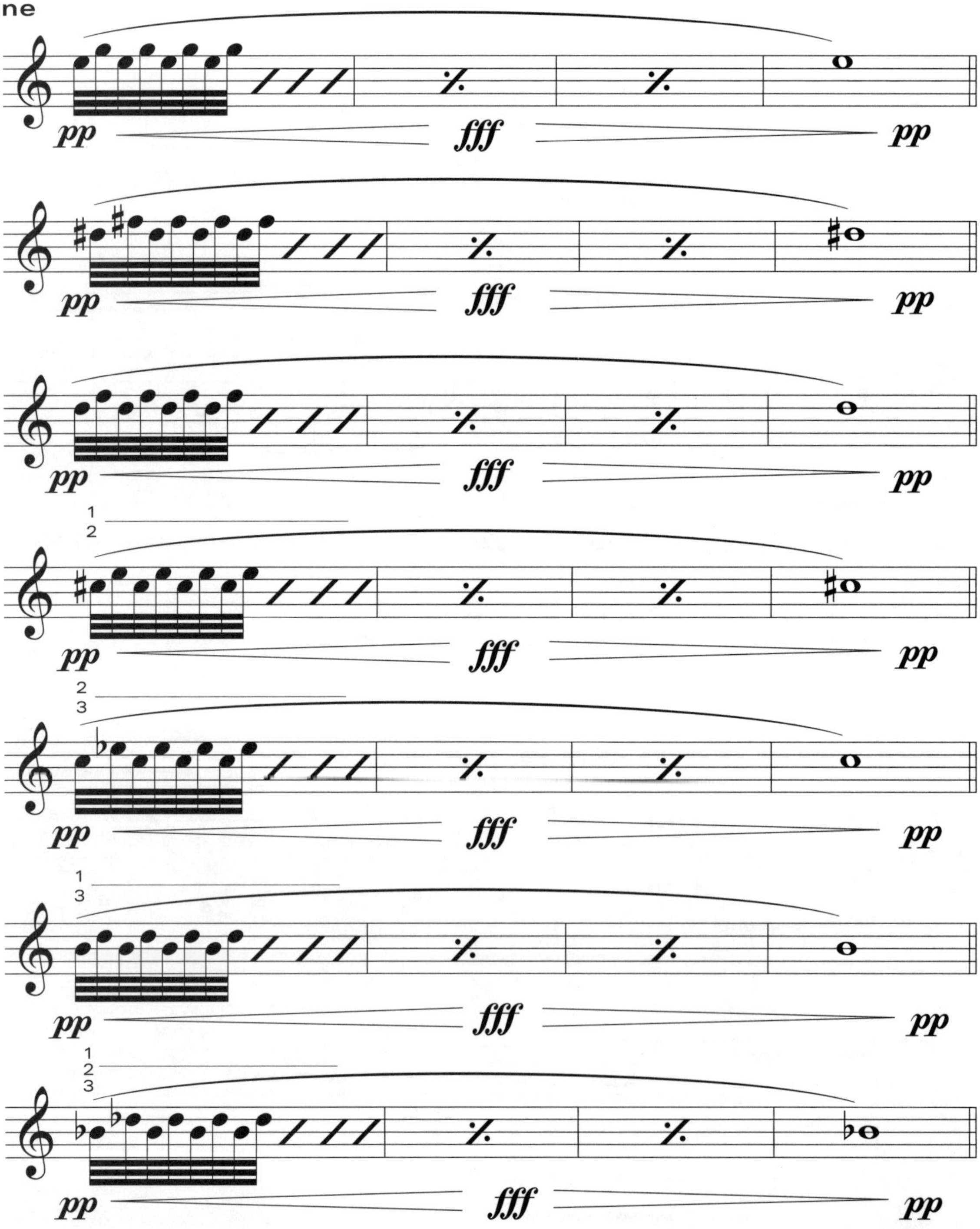

Two

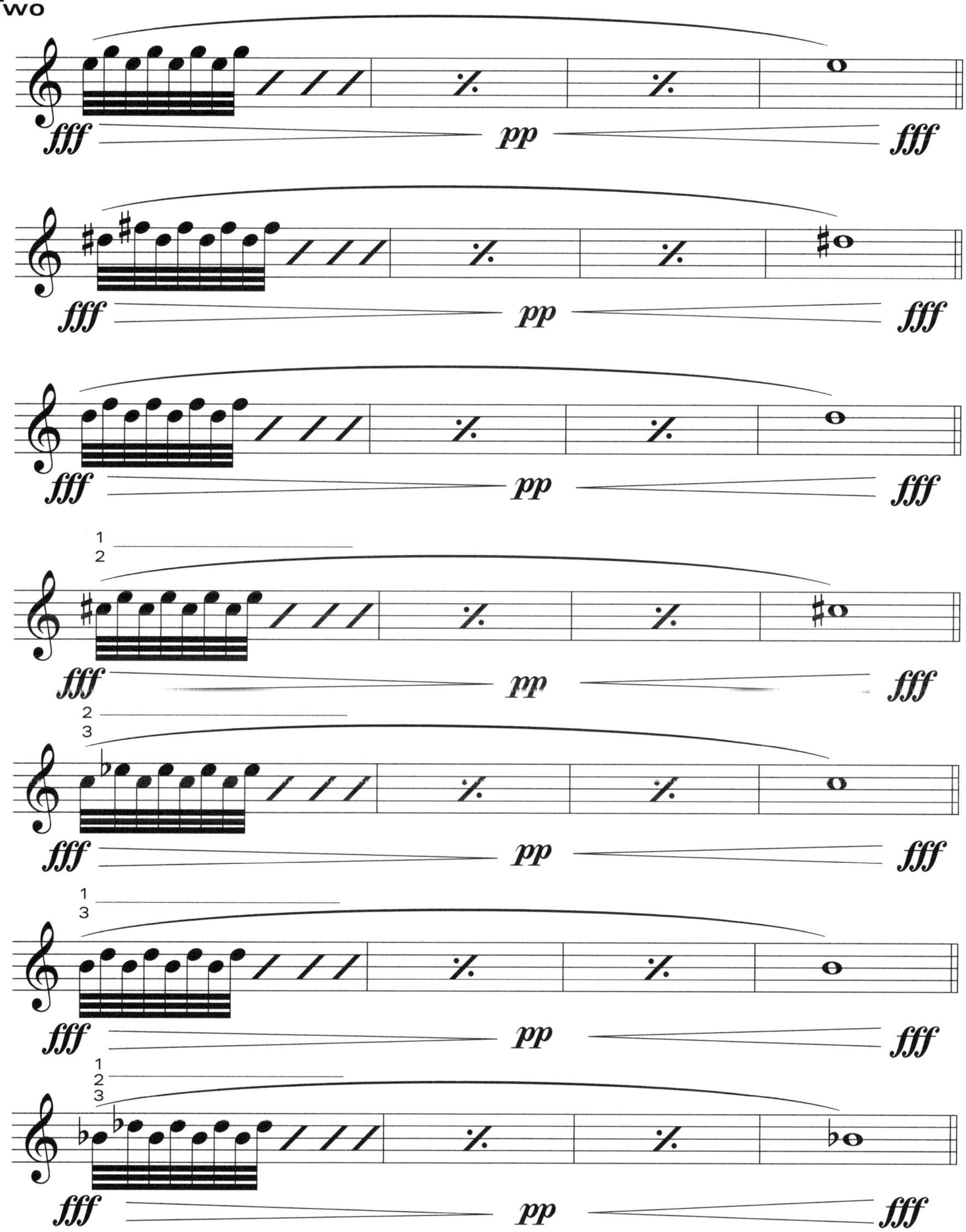

THREE • FLEXIBILITY

Three

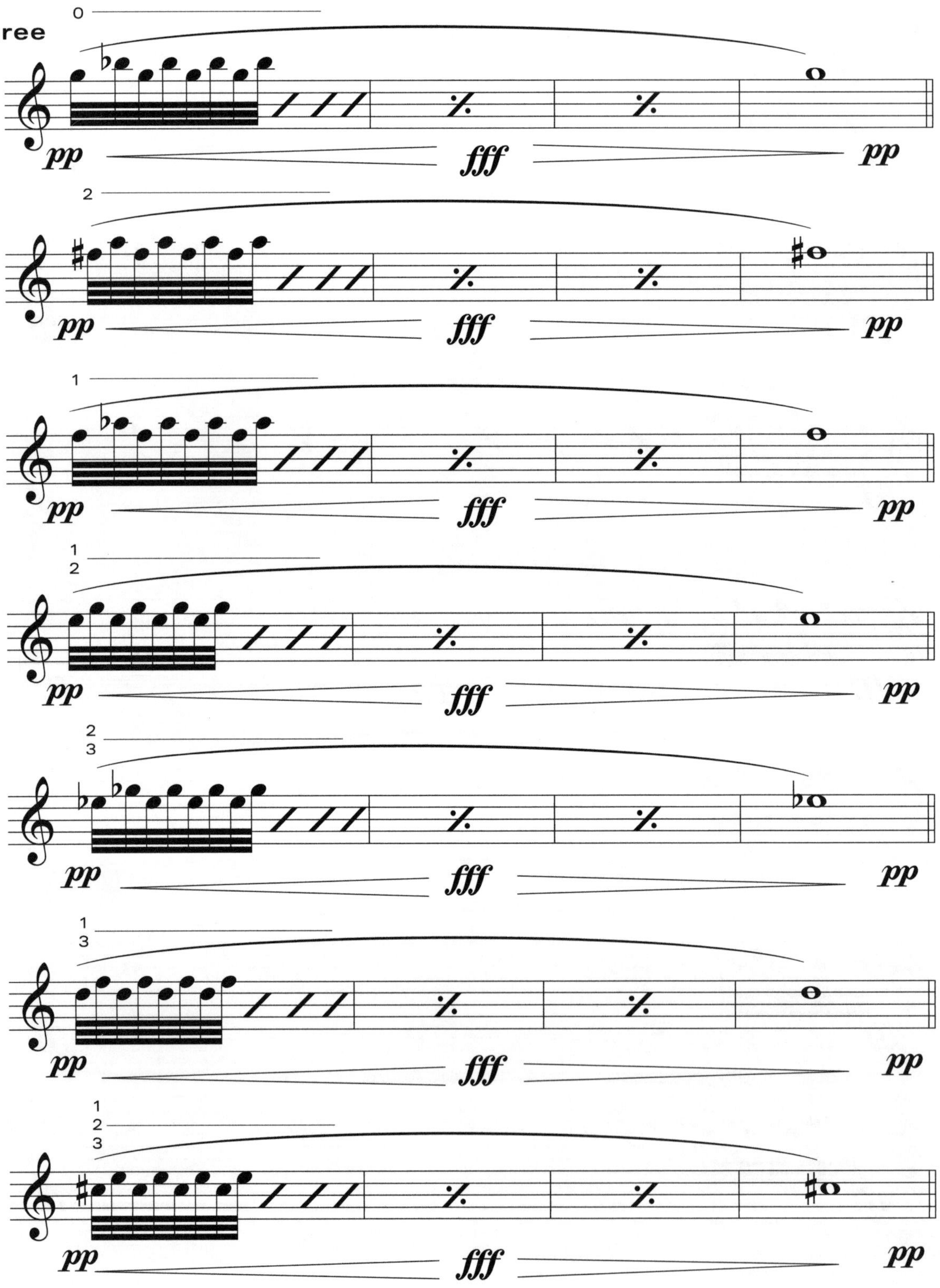

Four

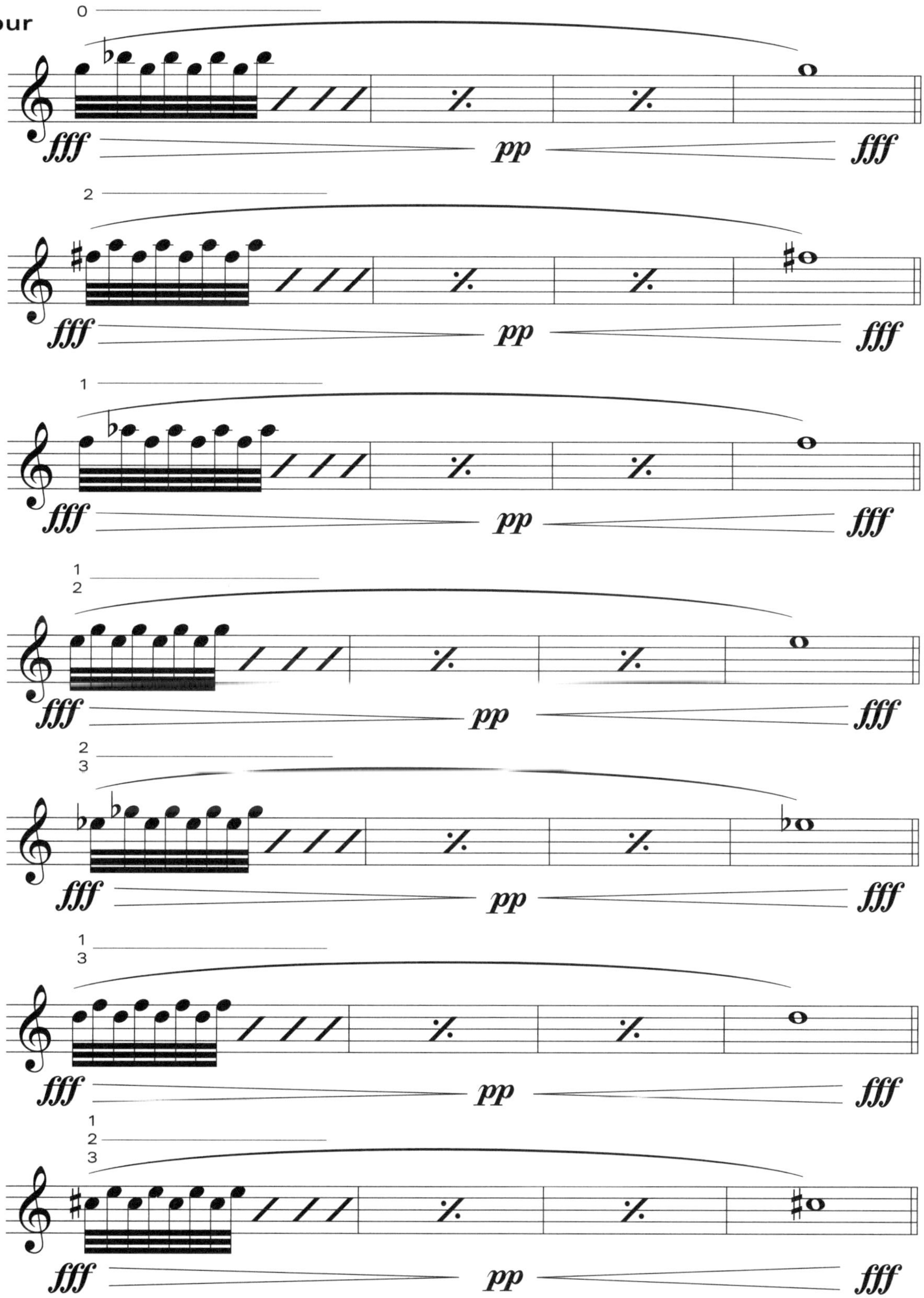
0
fff pp fff
2
fff pp fff
1
fff pp fff
1
2
fff pp fff
2
3
fff pp fff
1
3
fff pp fff
1
2
3
fff pp fff

THREE • FLEXIBILITY

These exercises involve two complimentary skills: 1) maintaining a pitch while moving the valves and 2) moving the pitch without using the valves. Practicing the material in this section will dramatically increase your flexibility in a very short time.

Begin by playing Exercises One and Seven several times each. When these can be played comfortably, add Exercises Two and Eight, then Three and Nine, etc. Eventually, exercises 14 through 23 should form a daily routine, with earlier exercises reviewed from time to time.

One

Maintain "E" pitch while fingering "F"

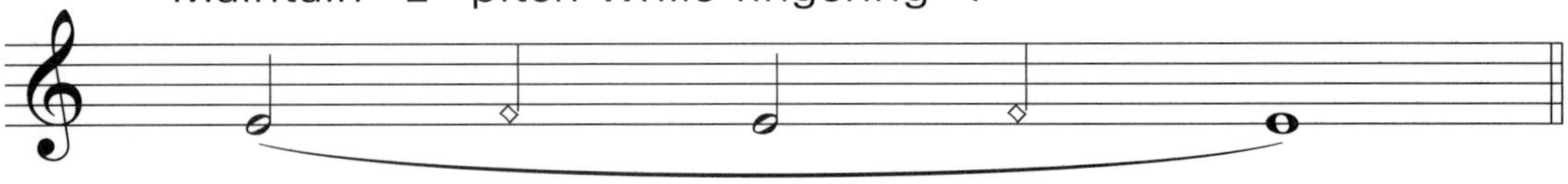

Two

Maintain "E" pitch throughout

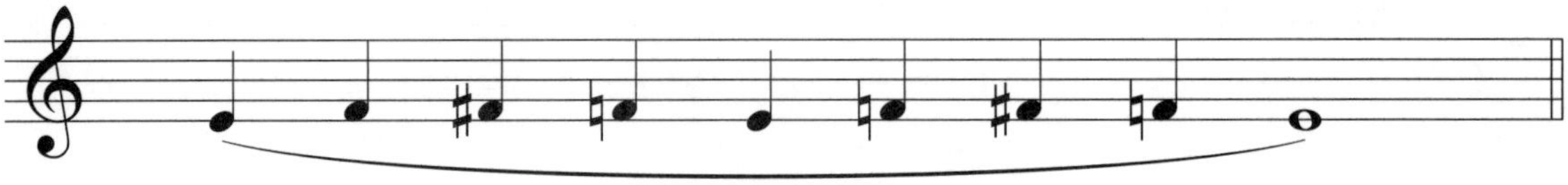

Three

Four

Maintain "A" pitch throughout

Five

Six

Seven

Lip Bend

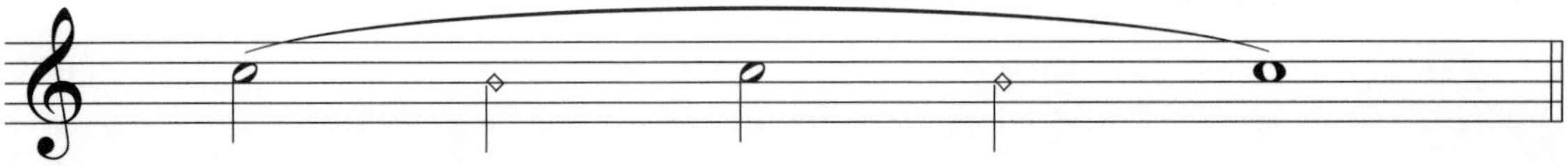

Eight

Nine

Ten

Eleven

Twelve

Thirteen

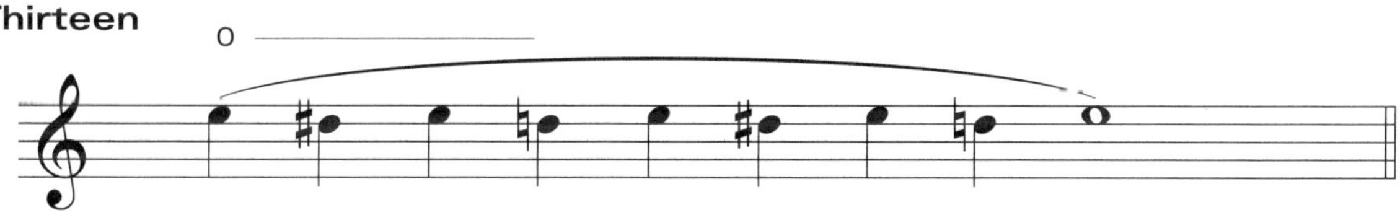

The following exercises are more advanced and require you to have mastered One through Thirteen.

Fourteen

Fifteen

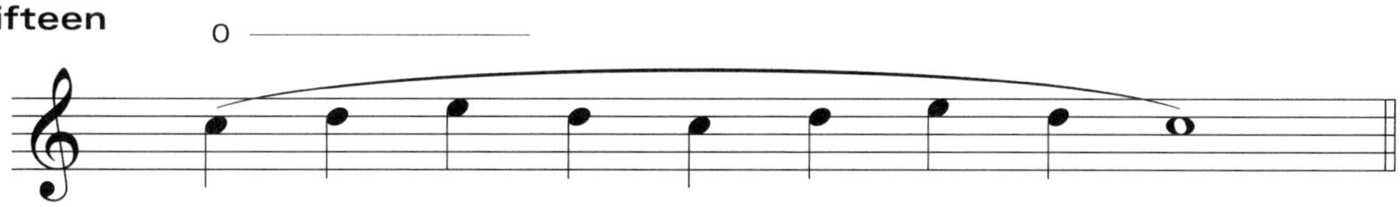

As soon as Fourteen and Fifteen can be attempted, they should be played every day.

Sixteen

Seventeen

Eighteen

Combine 19 through 23 with 14 and 15

Nineteen

Twenty

Twenty1

Twenty2

Twenty3

One

Finger E♭ major, but play D major

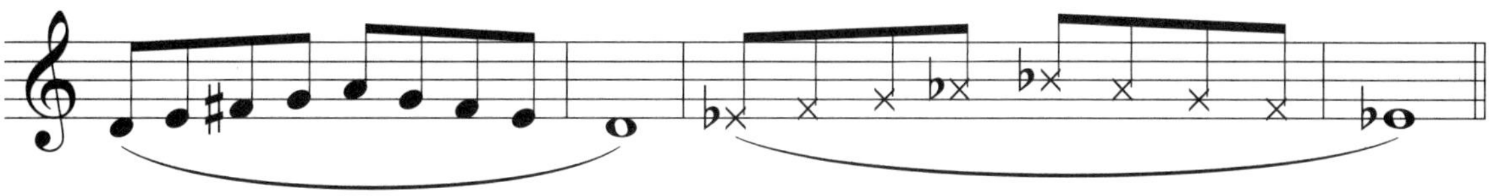

Finger F major, but play E major

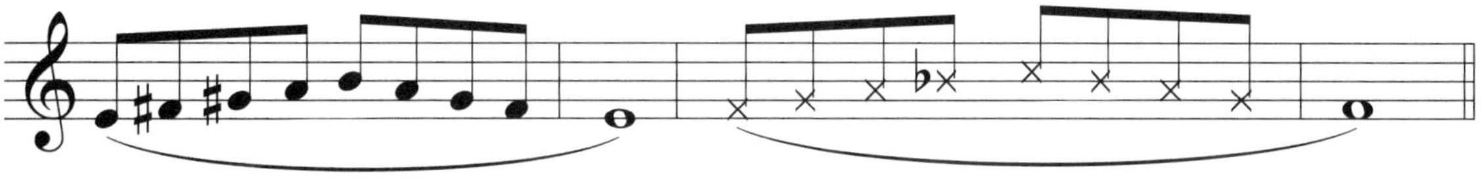

Two

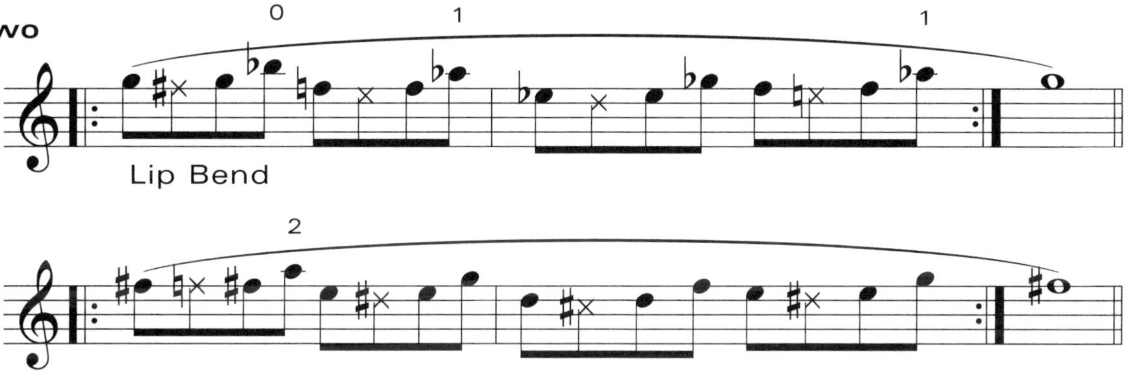

Three

FOUR • FLEXIBILITY

FOUR • INTERVAL STUDIES

The following exercises accustom you to slurring over consecutive fourths and fifths. Play each line several times without stopping. Try to maintain a steady airflow throughout.

One

Two

Three

Four

Five

ETUDE ONE

ETUDE TWO

ETUDE THREE

ETUDE • FLEXIBILITY

ARTICULATION

ONE • SLURRING/TONGUING

Trumpet players usually play more efficiently when slurring—the airstream is uninterrupted and there are fewer moving parts to coordinate. The tendency of many players is to have one tongue position and airstream for slurring and another for tonguing—in effect two completely different approaches to playing the trumpet. The exercises in this section are designed to develop a unified approach by juxtaposing slurring and tonguing. The slurred notes coordinate the action of lips and air. Then, while the pitch-producing motion continues, the tongue is added. The goal is to keep the identical setup and feel when slurring or tonguing.

Leave the mouthpiece on throughout. Breathe through the nose, adding as many beats rest as necessary.

Sometimes use legato tonguing, sometimes staccato.

One

1
2
BTN
BTN
BTN

ONE • ARTICULATION

Leave the mouthpiece on throughout. Breathe through the nose, adding as many beats rest as necessary.

Sometimes use legato tonguing, sometimes staccato.

Two

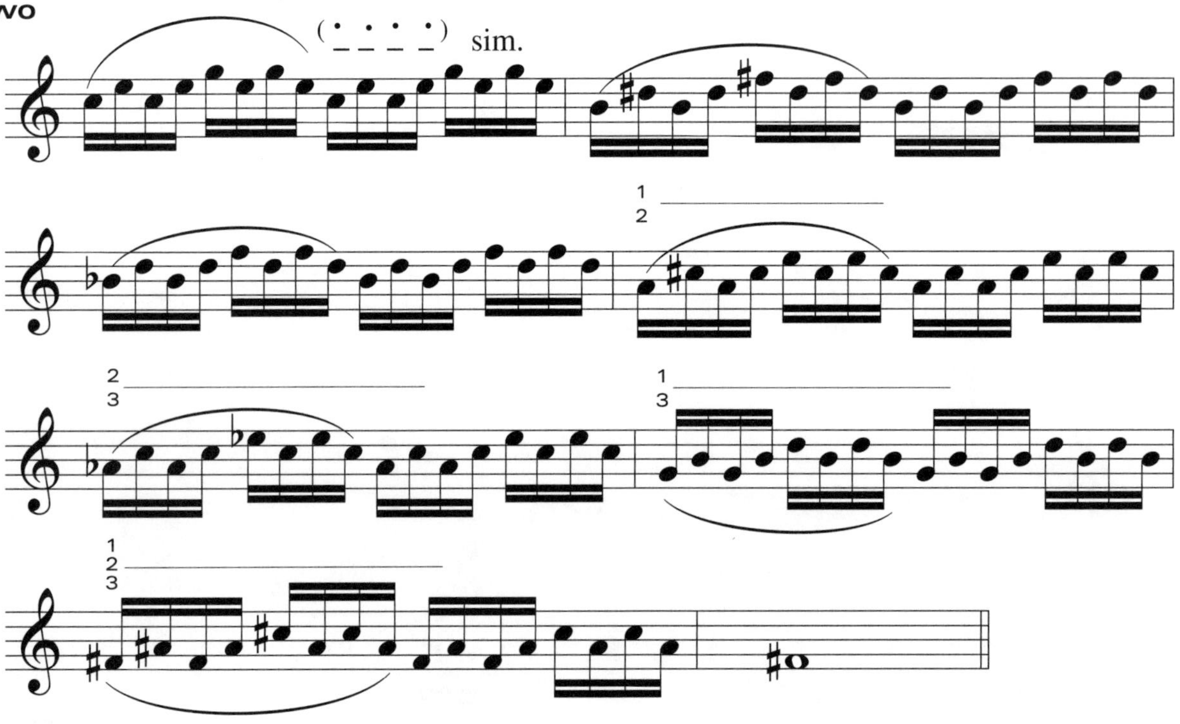

Three

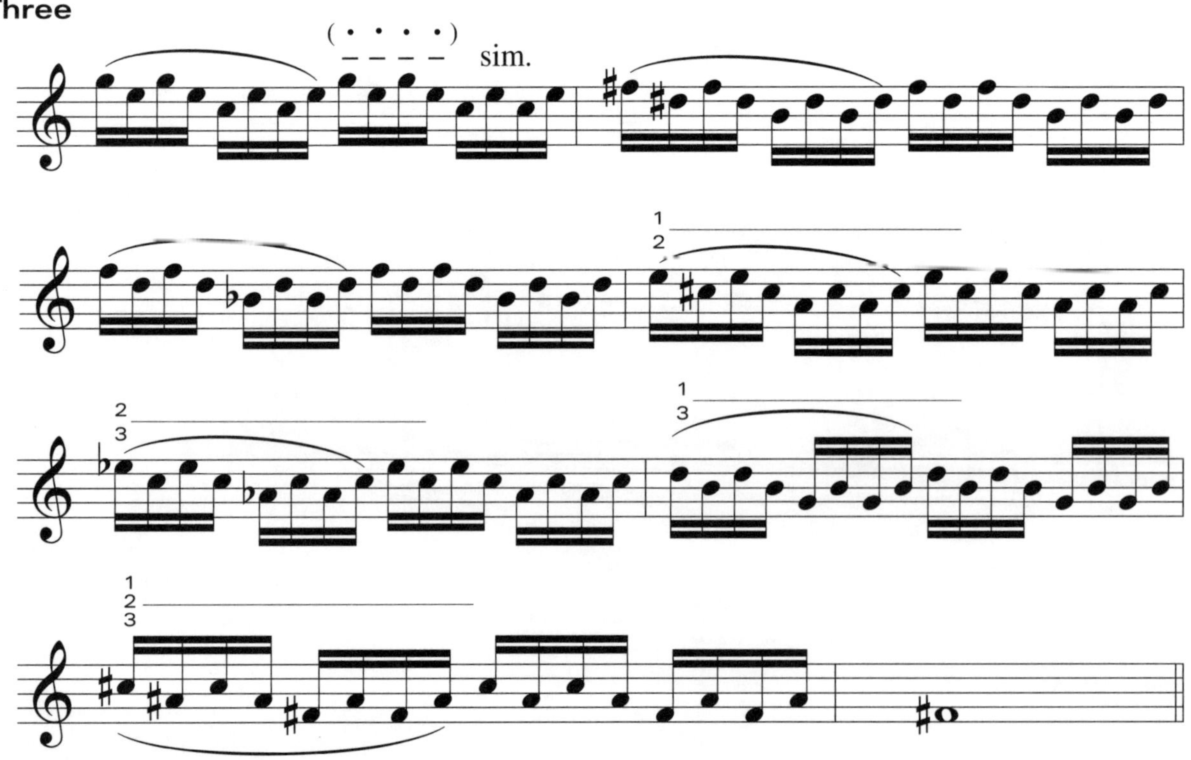

Leave the mouthpiece on throughout. Breathe through the nose, adding as many beats rest as necessary.

Sometimes use legato tonguing, sometimes staccato.

Four

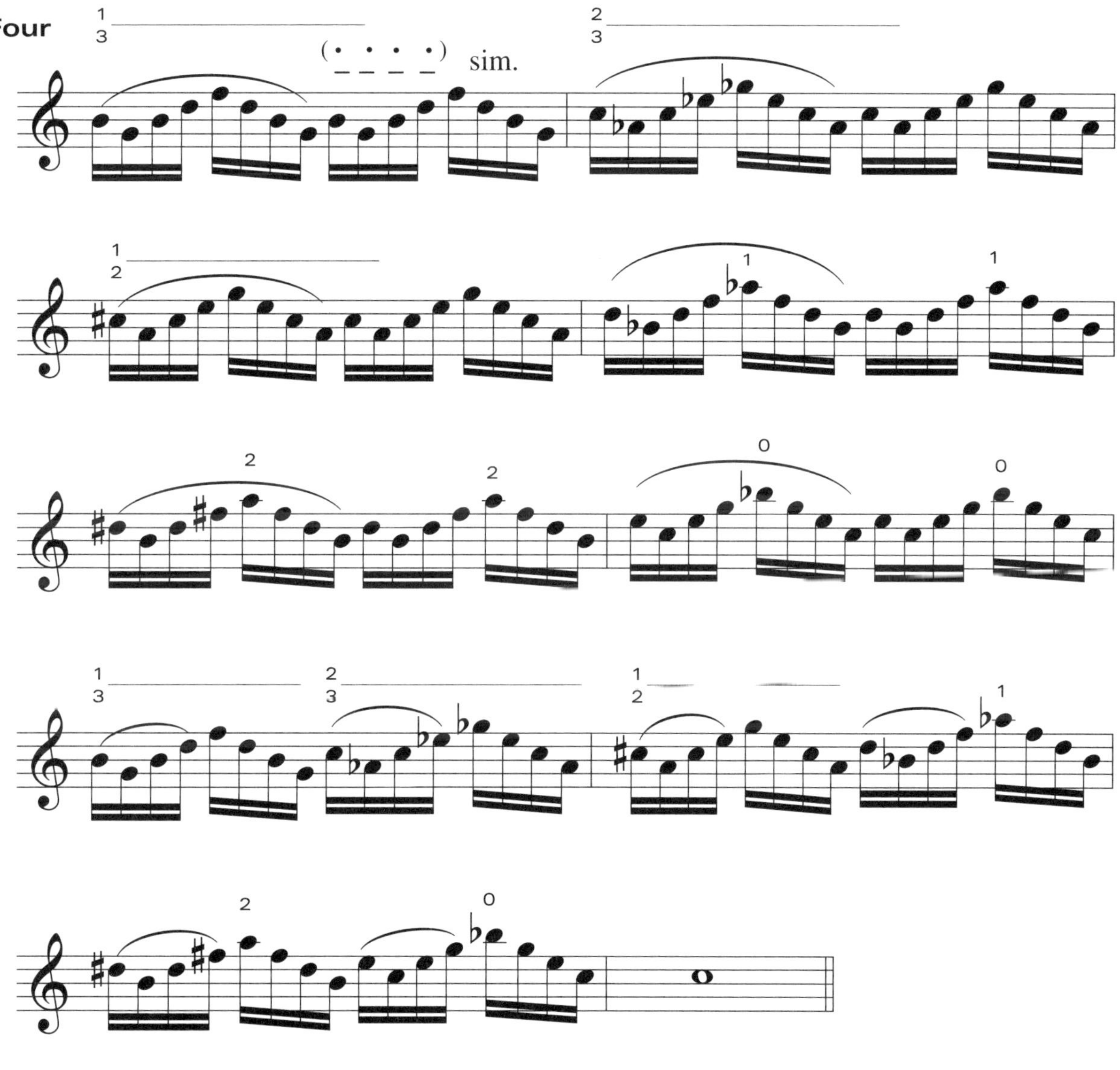

Reset after every line.

Sometimes use legato tonguing, sometimes staccato.

Five

ETUDE FOUR

TWO • ARTICULATION

TWO • DEVELOPED SCALE

The following exercises are written with a C Dorian mode but should be applied to as many scale types as possible. If these exercises are too strenuous as written, reverse direction at G on top of the staff or play the entire exercise in a lower key. Exercises One through Ten extend the Developed Scale to the interval of a 5th. It should be further extended through 6ths, 7ths and octaves. Play only one exercise from this section in any one day.

Leave the mouthpiece on throughout. Breathe through the nose, adding as many beats rest as necessary. Use legato tonguing unless otherwise indicated.

One

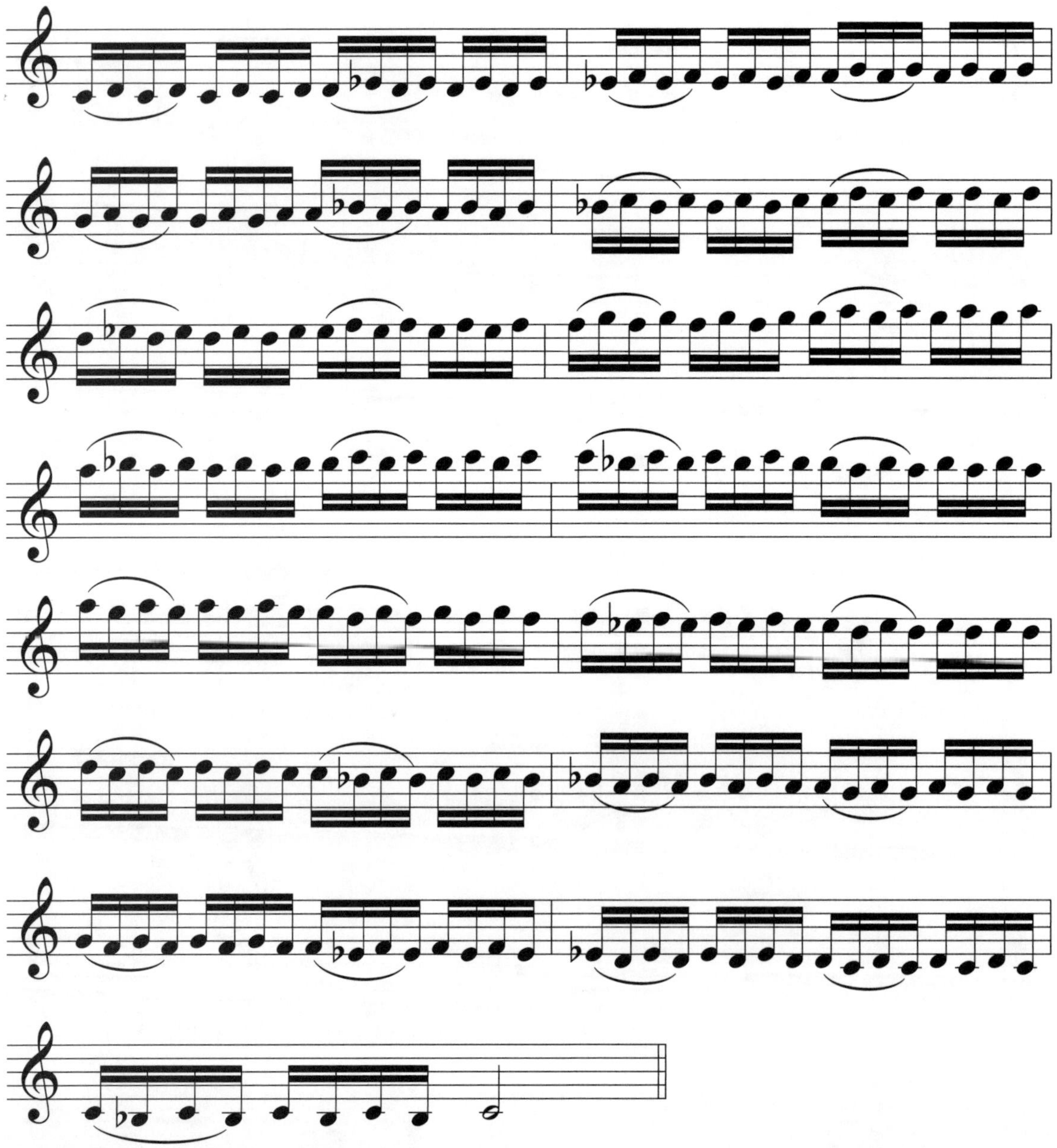

Play the previous exercise with each of the following variations:

In the following variations, exaggerate the accents.

When playing four consecutive tongued notes, introduce this variation as well:

TWO • ARTICULATION

Leave the mouthpiece on throughout. Breathe through the nose, adding as many beats rest as necessary.

Two

Play the previous exercise with each of the following variations:

TWO • ARTICULATION

Leave the mouthpiece on throughout. Breathe through the nose, adding as many beats rest as necessary.

Three

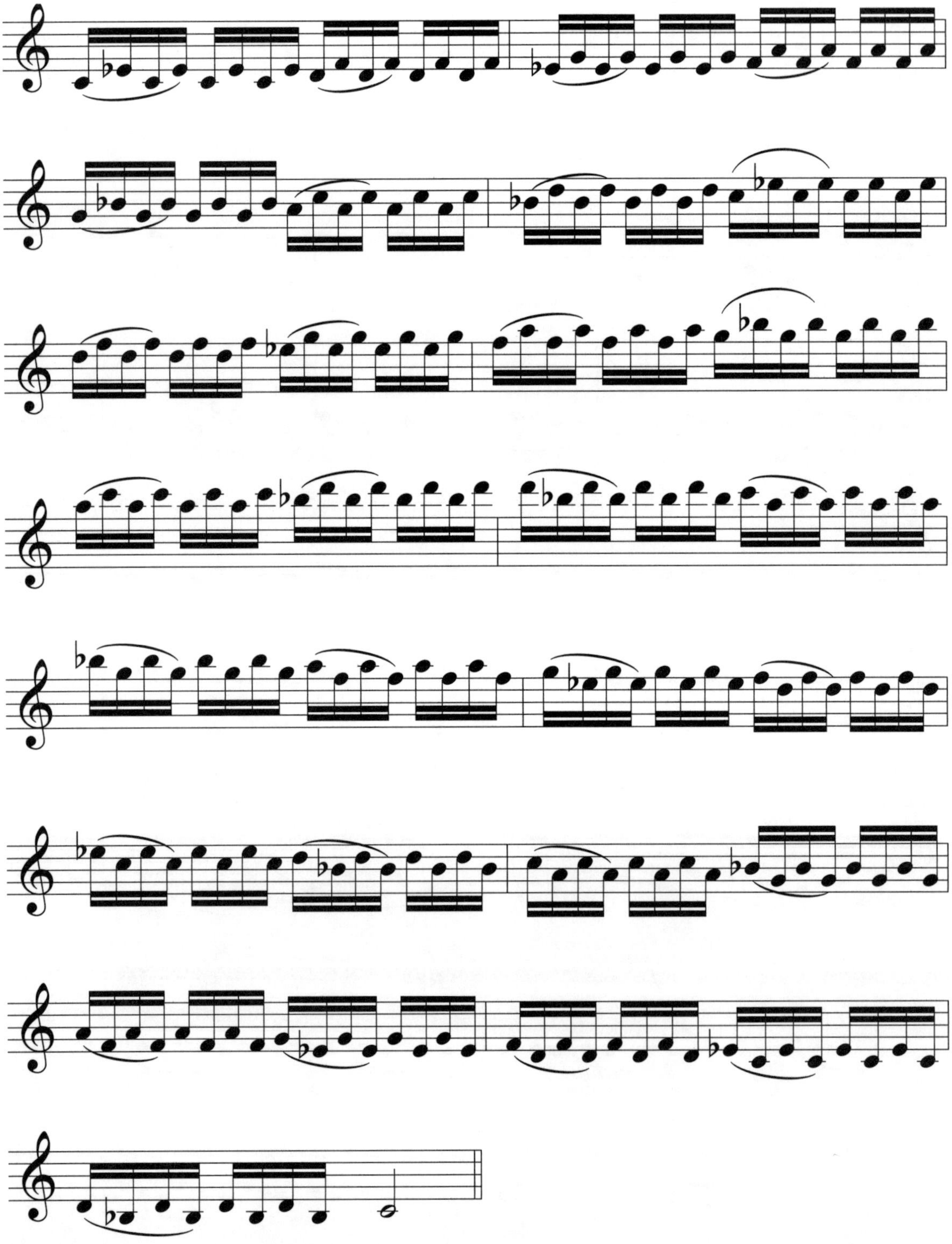

Play the previous exercise with each of the following variations:

When playing four consecutive tongued notes, introduce this variation as well:

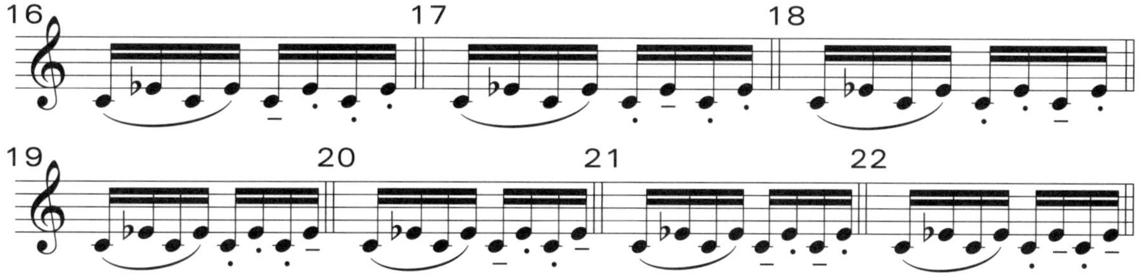

TWO • ARTICULATION

The following exercise and its variations combine Exercises Two and Three.
Leave the mouthpiece on throughout. Breathe through the nose, adding as many beats rest as necessary.

Four

Etc.

Variation I

Variation II

Variation III

Five

Continue sequence up to:

Cont. sequence down to:

Play the previous exercise with each of the following variations:

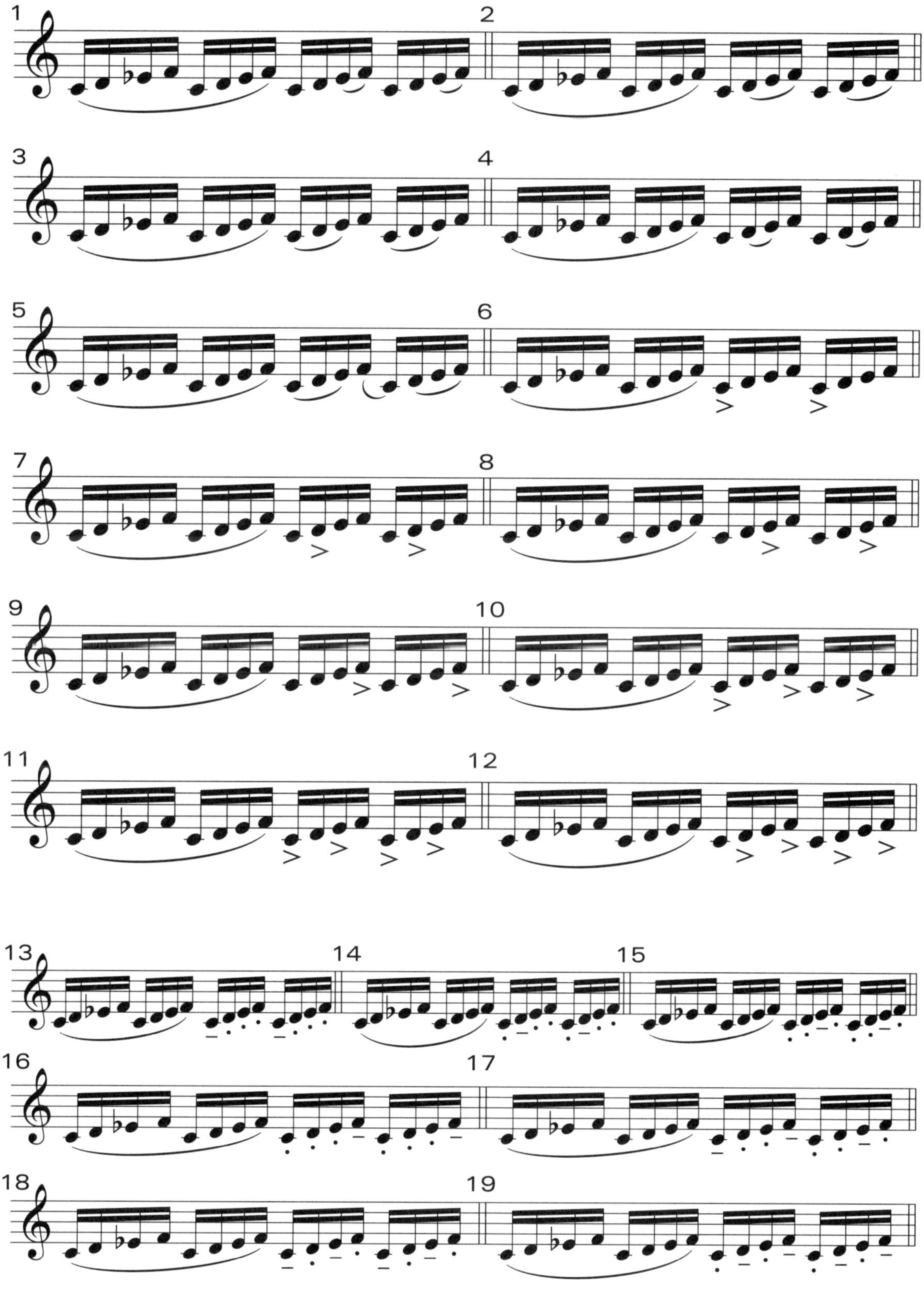

TWO • ARTICULATION

Six

Leave the mouthpiece on throughout. Breathe through the nose, adding as many beats rest as necessary.

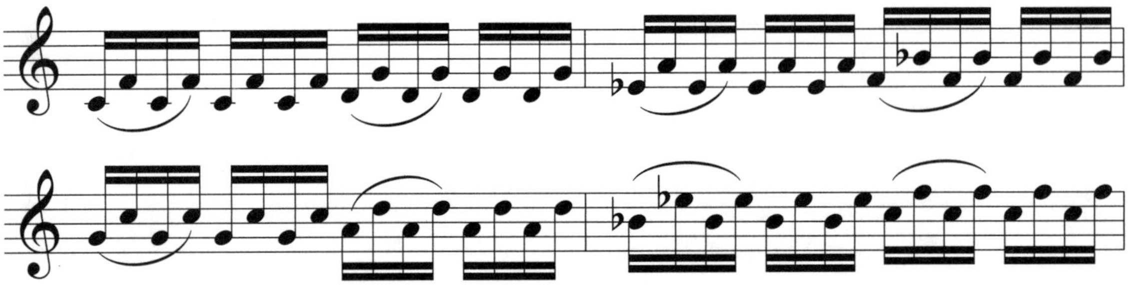

Continue sequence up to:

Cont. sequence down to:

Play the previous exercise with each of the following variations:

7 8

9 10

11 12

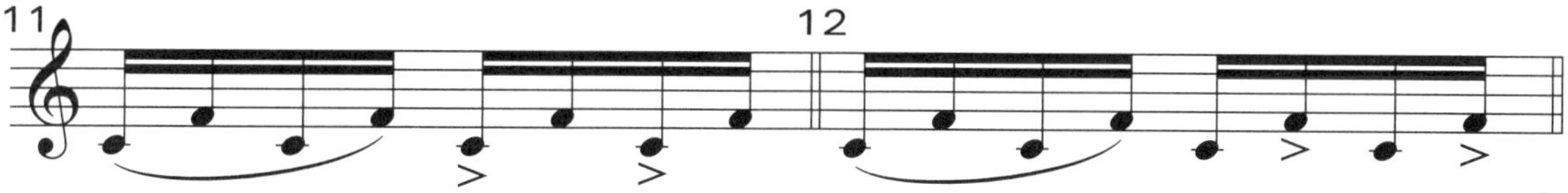

13 14 15

16 17 18 19

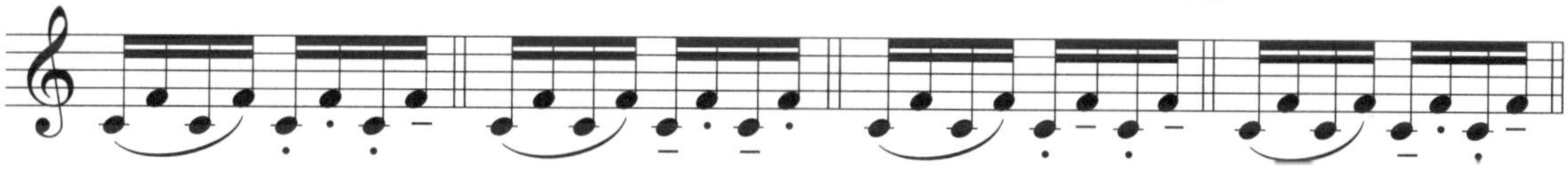

The following exercise and its variations combine Exercises Five and Six.
Leave the mouthpiece on throughout. Breathe through the nose, adding as many beats rest as necessary.

Seven

Etc.

Variation I Variation II

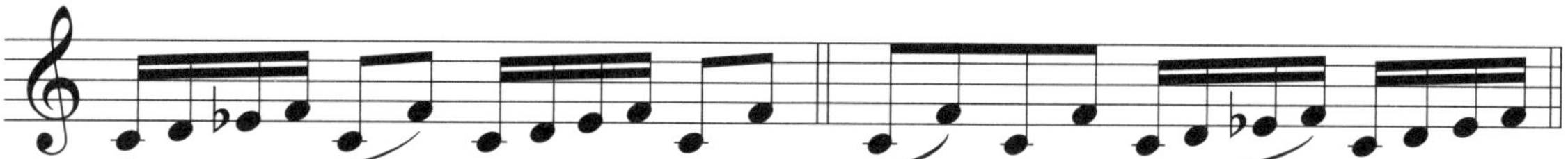

Variation III

TWO • ARTICULATION

Eight Leave the mouthpiece on throughout. Breathe through the nose, adding as many beats rest as necessary.

Continue sequence up to:

Cont. sequence down to:

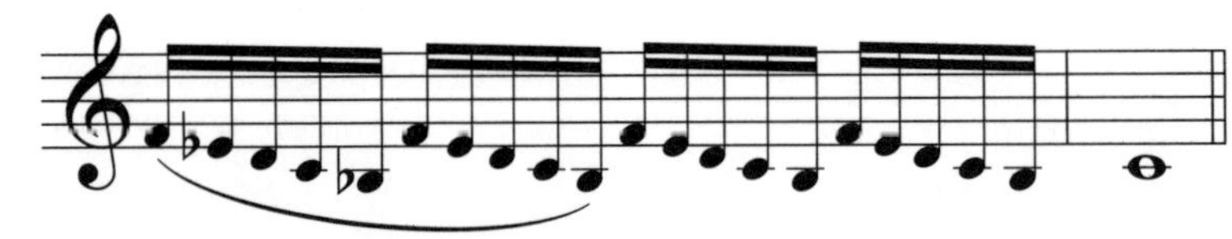

Play the previous exercise with each of the following variations:

1 2

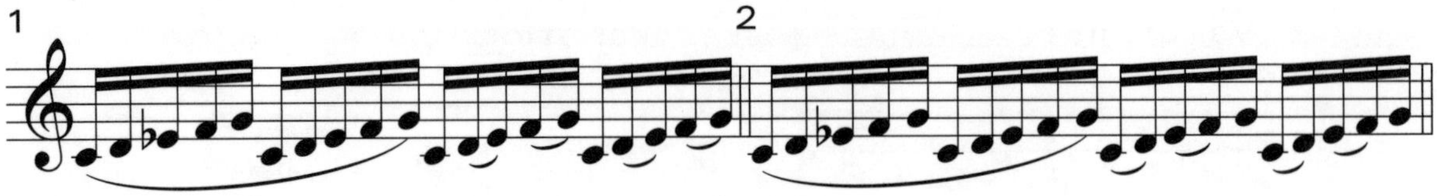

3 4

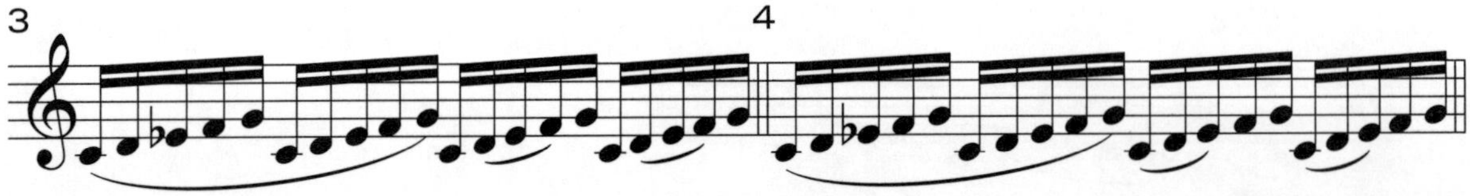

Nine

Continue sequence up to:

Cont. sequence down to:

The following exercise and its variations combine Exercises Eight and Nine.

Leave the mouthpiece on throughout. Breathe through the nose, adding as many beats rest as necessary.

Ten

Etc.

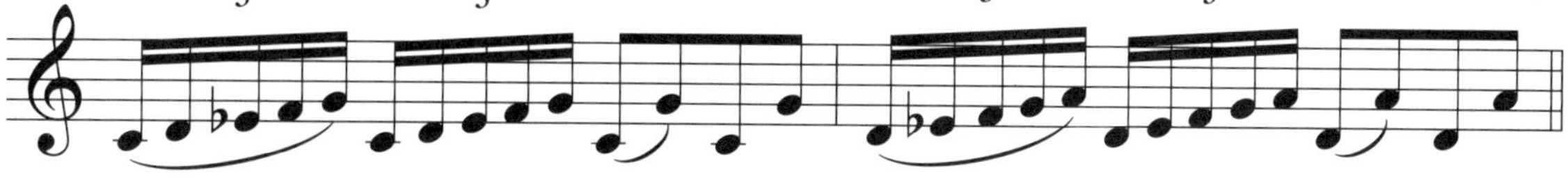

Variation I

Variation II

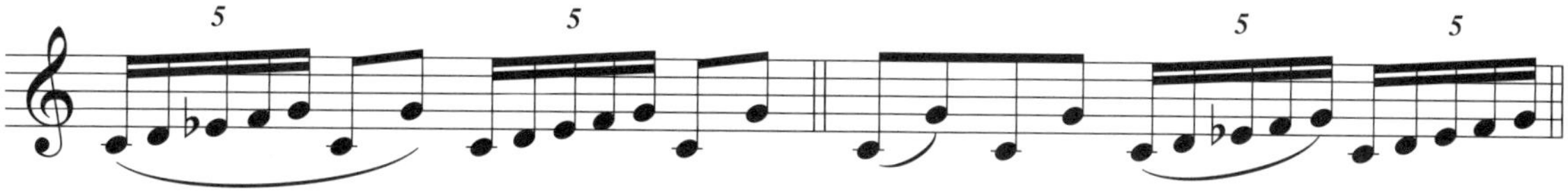

Variation III

Exercise Eleven should be played in tandem with a Developed Scale exercise. The goal is to produce an A above the staff efficiently and then maintain the same feel and sound while approaching the A from progressively lower degrees. A above the staff is significantly different in timbre from G a whole step below and generally feels like the beginning of the upper register.

Ultimately this entire exercise should be played with one setting; however, begin by removing the mouthpiece from the lips and resting after every two or three lines.

Eleven

Continued...

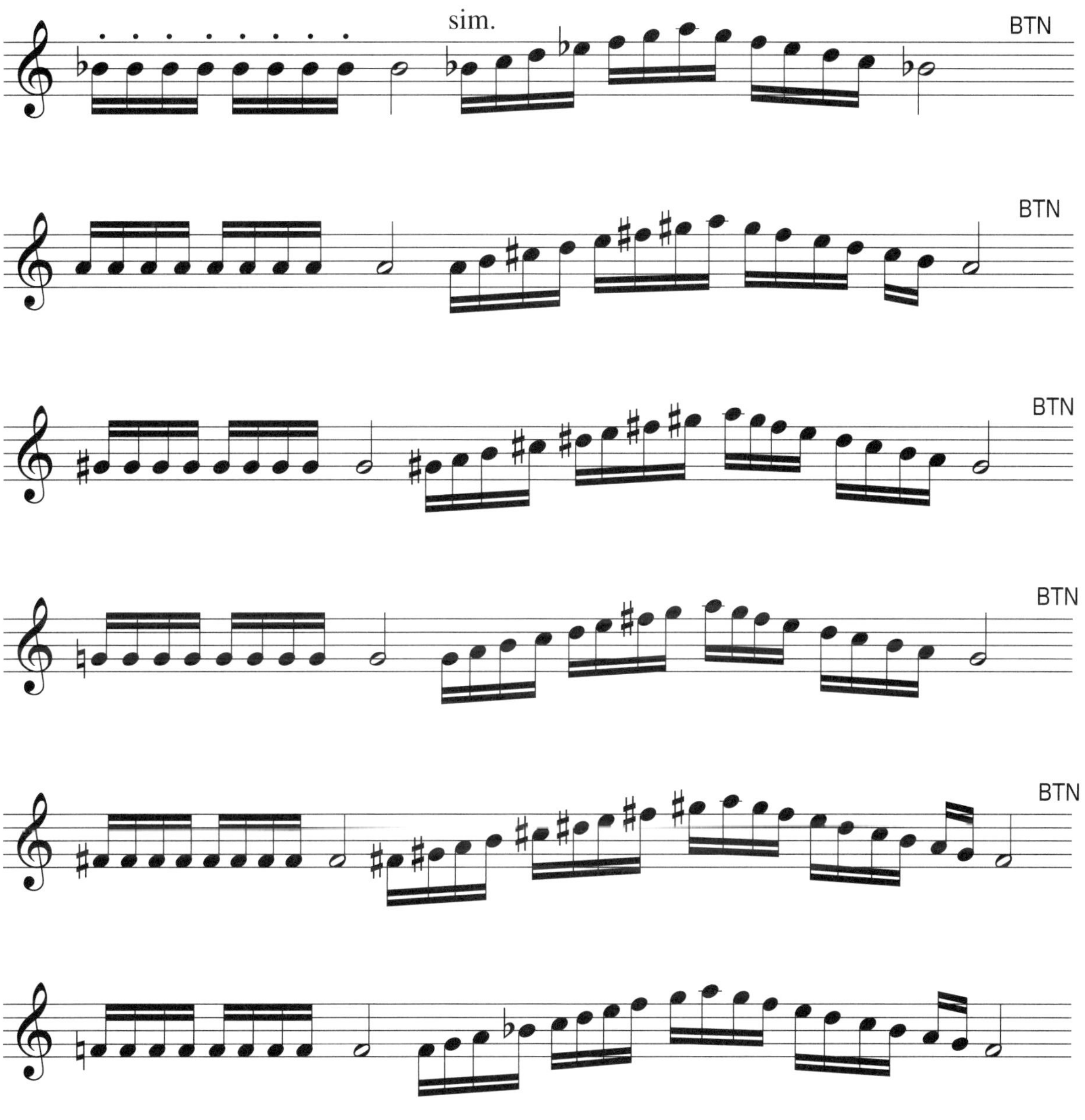
sim.
BTN
BTN
BTN
BTN
BTN

THREE • ARTICULATION

THREE • ARPEGGIOS/DIRECTION CHANGES

Leave the mouthpiece on throughout each exercise. Breathe through the nose, adding as many beats rest as necessary. The first line should be slurred the first time and tongued on the repeat.

One Slur 1st x, tongue 2nd x

Two Slur 1st x, tongue 2nd x

Leave the mouthpiece on throughout. Breathe through the nose, adding as many beats rest as necessary.

Three Slur 1st x, tongue 2nd x

Four Slur 1st x, tongue 2nd x

THREE • ARTICULATION

Leave the mouthpiece on throughout. Breathe through the nose, adding as many beats rest as necessary.

Five Slur 1st x, tongue 2nd x

Six Slur 1st x, tongue 2nd x

Leave the mouthpiece on throughout. Breathe through the nose, adding as many beats rest as necessary.

Seven Slur 1st x, tongue 2nd x

Eight Slur 1st x, tongue 2nd x

Nine Slur 1st x, tongue 2nd x

Ten Slur 1st x, tongue 2nd x

Eleven Slur 1st x, tongue 2nd x

Twelve Slur 1st x, tongue 2nd x

Thirteen

Fourteen

Whether slurring or tonguing, repeated changes in direction are very challenging to execute. Learn to execute Exercises One through Four before attempting Exercises Five through Eight.

Slur each exercise at least twice, then single tongue it several times.

One

Two

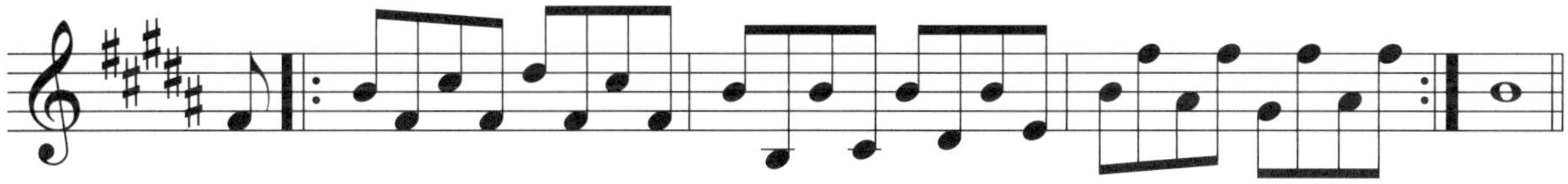

Three

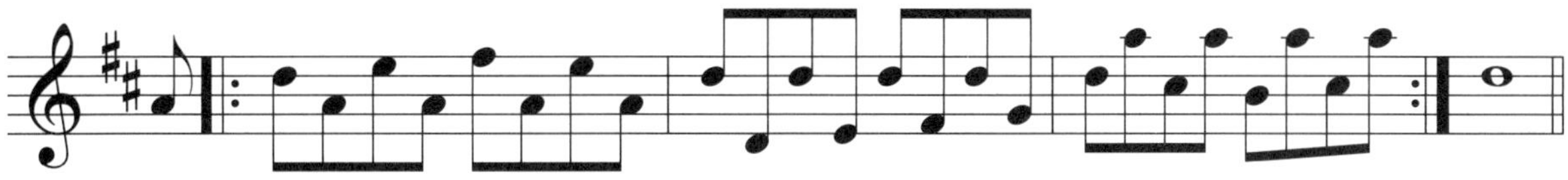

Four

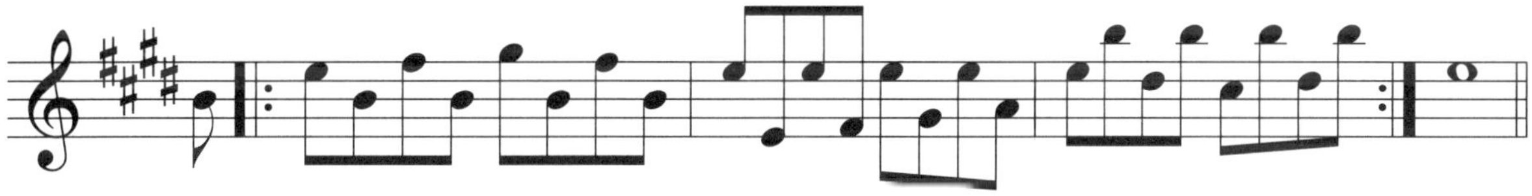

Five

Six

Seven

Eight

ETUDE FIVE

ARTICULATION • ETUDE

PEDAL TONES

Pedal tones can be a useful addition to any trumpet routine. They aid in relaxation and reinforce the concept that the lips—not the instrument—form the notes. Because pedal tones increase the flow of blood to the lips, they also help to reduce swelling and relieve stiffness on the day following a strenuous performance. They can be used as a warm down immediately after a performance as well.

Overuse of pedal tones can have negative effects. Symptoms such as a flabby, dead tone, poor intonation, and loss of range or flexibility are the cue to suspend pedal tone practice and seek the advice of a teacher. With the exception of the Preparatory Exercise, it is important to practice only one pedal tone exercise in a given day.

Since pedal tones can change mouthpiece placement and jaw position, they should be immediately followed by a scale that covers most of the range of the instrument. This refocuses the embouchure and teaches the body to maintain the relaxation of the pedal register when moving into the upper register, resulting in increased range and endurance. Pedal tones should be played in the middle of a practice session, since playing them at the beginning can confuse the embouchure.

Practicing Pedal Tones:

1. Play each exercise slowly.
2. Use Long Setting.
3. Play at a mezzo-forte dynamic.
4. Descend as low as possible, allowing the mouthpiece to move wherever it wants.
5. Fingerings are optional—use whatever fingerings are easiest.

The following pedal tone exercise can be used as a warm down at the end of a practice day or performance. This particular exercise can be used freely in conjunction with other pedal tone exercises. If you have trouble producing pitches in the pedal register, this exercise will help develop that skill.

Leave the mouthpiece on throughout. Breathe through the nose, adding as many beats rest as necessary.

Preparatory Exercise

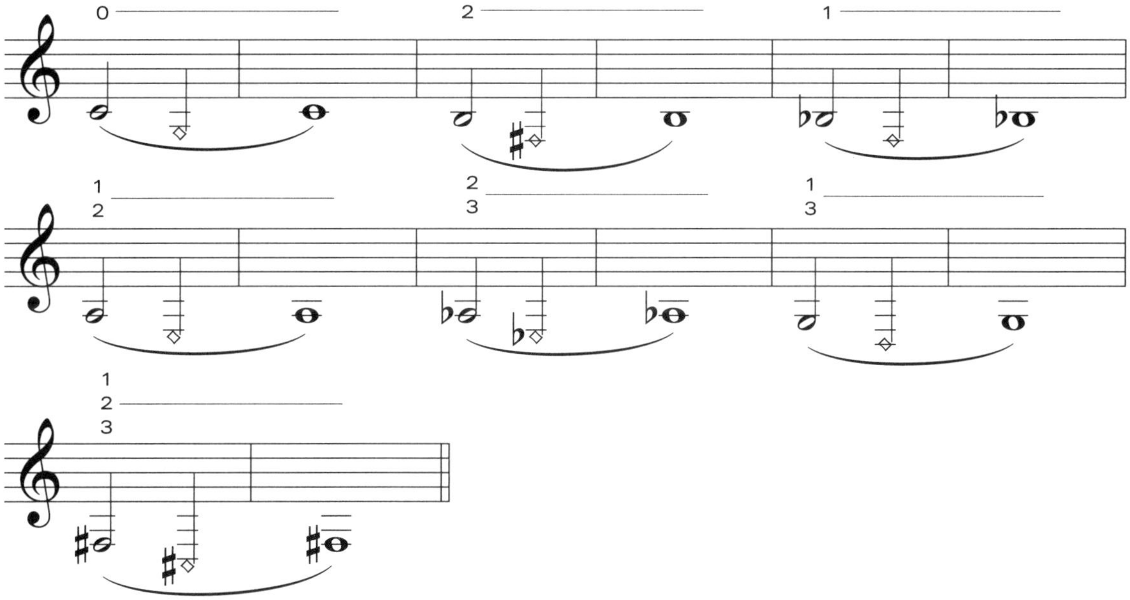

One

Continue the pattern down chromatically as far as possible. Reset and conclude with the following scale:

PEDAL TONES

Leave the mouthpiece on throughout. Breathe through the nose, adding as many beats rest as necessary.

Two

Continue exercise as high as possible

Three

Continue exercise as high as possible

PEDAL TONES

Leave the mouthpiece on throughout. Breathe through the nose, adding as many beats rest as necessary.

One

Repeat 3 or 4 times

Two

Repeat 3 or 4 times

Three

Repeat 3 or 4 times

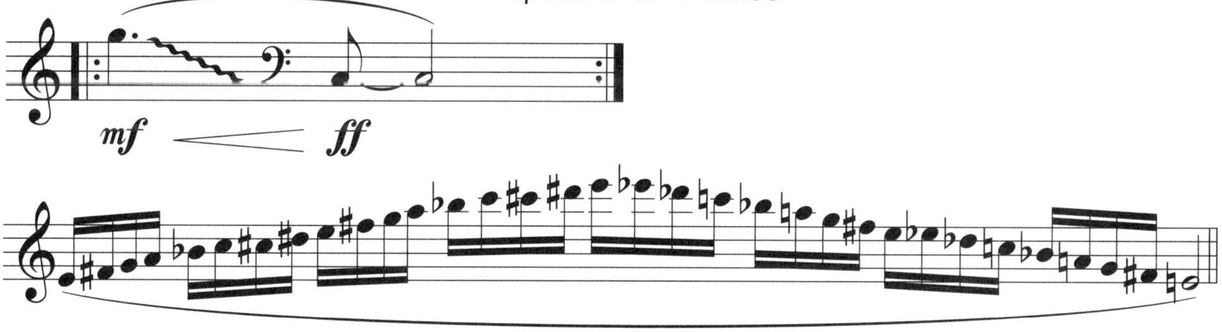

Four

Repeat 3 or 4 times

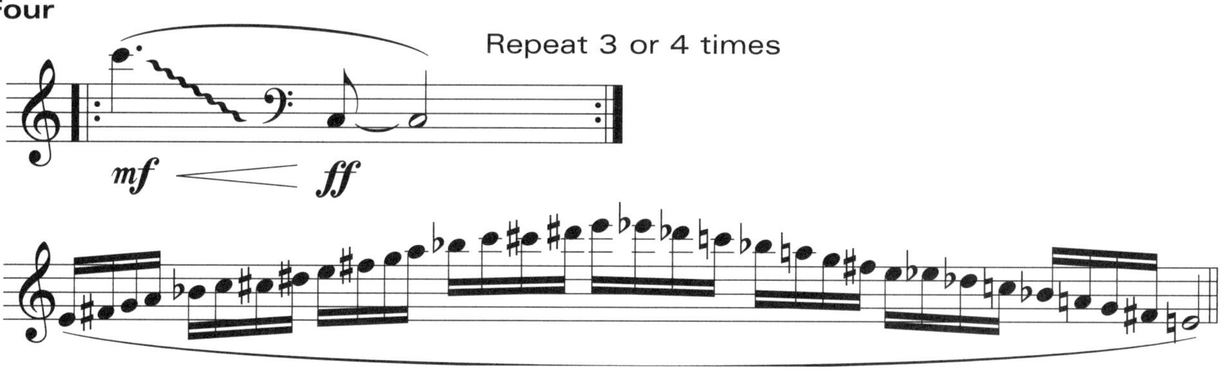

PEDAL TONES

Leave the mouthpiece on throughout. Breathe through the nose, adding as many beats rest as necessary.

One

Continue down the harmonic series to low F♯.

Two

Continue down the harmonic series to low F♯.

Three

Continue down the harmonic series to low F♯.

Four

Continue down the harmonic series to low F♯.

Five

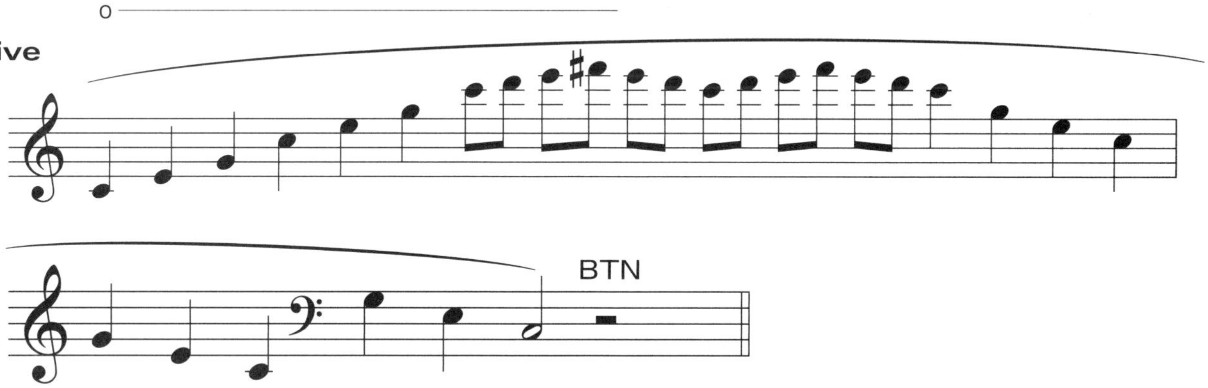

Continue down the harmonic series to low F♯.

Six

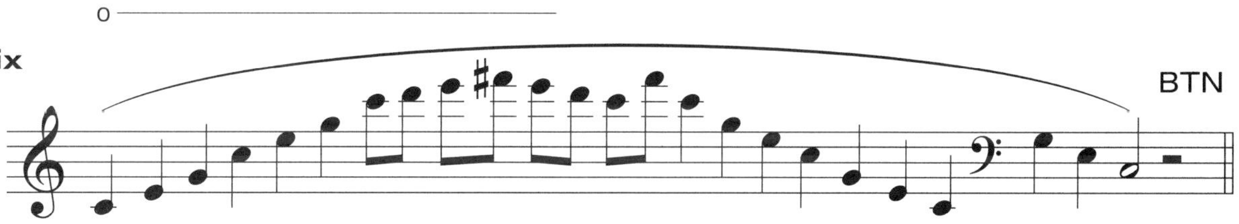

Continue down the harmonic series to low F♯.

Seven

Continue down the harmonic series to low F♯.

The pattern established by these exercises should be continued as high as possible.

QUICK

REGISTER CHANGES

ONE • CONSISTENT INTERVALS

The prevalence of wide intervals and angular melodic lines in contemporary music makes it absolutely necessary to be able to shift registers quickly and efficiently. However, changing registers quickly is probably the hardest thing to do on the trumpet. Many factors such as air speed, tongue position, lip tension, etc., must be coordinated in order to do this effectively and without embouchure distortion or extraneous motion.

The initial exercises in this section gradually accustom the embouchure to rapid changes in register through the use of consistent intervals. Exercises One through Eleven, pages 90 through 93, are built around diminished seventh chords, which divide the octave evenly into minor thirds. The exercises on pages 94 through 97 are based on augmented triads, which divide the octave evenly into major thirds. Practicing these exercises will help you develop a fluid connection between registers.

One

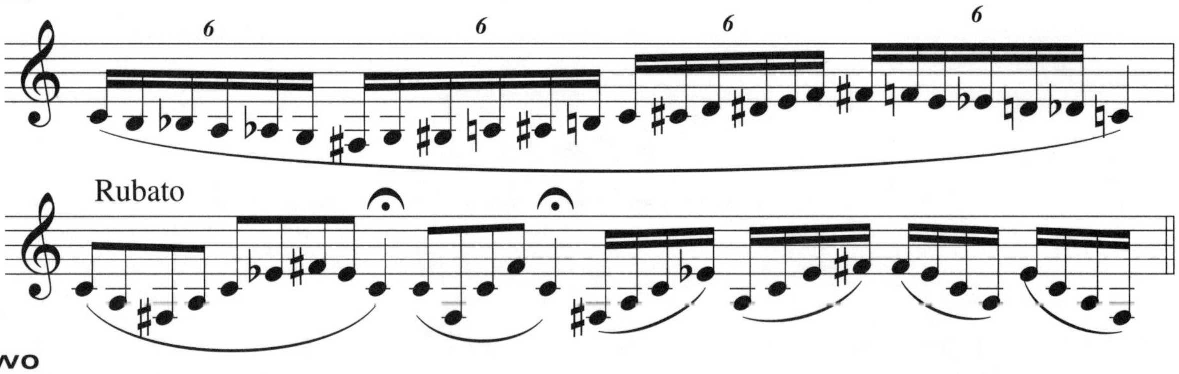

Two

Three

Four

Five

Six

ONE • QUICK REGISTER CHANGES

Seven

Eight

Nine

Ten

Transpose the pattern ascending chromatically. On the tritones and diminished arpeggios, descend to the lowest chord tone possible. Eventually, arrive at this final version:

Eleven

ONE • QUICK REGISTER CHANGES

One

Two

Three

Four

Five

Six

Seven

Eight

Nine

Transpose the pattern ascending chromatically. On all arpeggios, descend to the lowest chord tone possible.

TWO • SPIDERS

These exercises are Long Setting. Breathe through the nose, adding as many beats rest as necessary. Practice the first part of each exercise (up to the coda sign) until it can be played comfortably; then add the coda, resetting in between. Keep a continuous air stream through the center point of each line.

Exercises Seven, Eight and Nine are based on Diminished Scales. Exercises Ten and Eleven are based on Whole Tone Scales. Twelve is based on a C Major Pentatonic Scale.

Begin at ♩ = 60; double time when comfortable.

One

Two Slur throughout

Three Slur throughout

TWO • QUICK REGISTER CHANGES

Four Slur throughout

Five Slur throughout

Six Slur throughout

(Exercises 7 through 9 are based on diminished scales)

Seven Slur throughout

TWO • QUICK REGISTER CHANGES

Eight Slur throughout

Nine Slur throughout

QUICK REGISTER CHANGES • TWO

(Exercises 10 and 11 are based on whole tone scales)

Ten Slur throughout

Eleven Slur throughout

Twelve Slur throughout (Exercise 12 is based on a pentatonic scale)

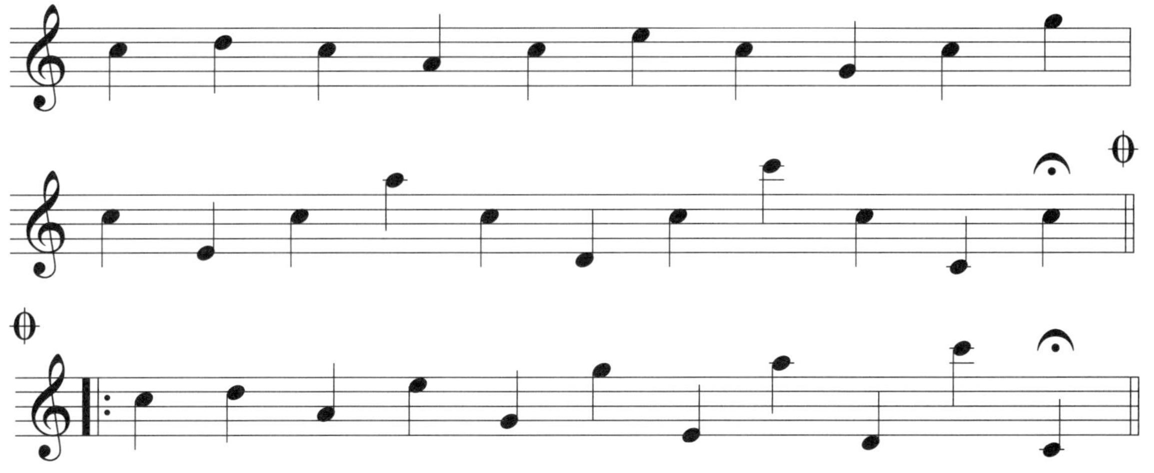

ETUDE • QUICK REGISTER CHANGES

ETUDE SIX

QUICK REGISTER CHANGES • ETUDE

THREE • QUICK REGISTER CHANGES

THREE • CHROMATIC DISPLACEMENT

These studies are designed to connect the registers, resulting in freer movement throughout the entire range of the instrument. Exercise One should be practiced for at least one week before adding Exercise Two. Both exercises should be practiced for at least a week before adding Exercise Three, etc. As execution improves, additional exercises should be added. When pages 106 through 112 can be executed comfortably, make selected exercises part of a daily routine.

Do each exercise three times:

♪ = 90 ♪ = 180 ♪ = 360

Leave the mouthpiece on throughout. Breathe through the nose, adding as many beats rest as necessary. Reset for each tempo change.

One

Two Slur throughout

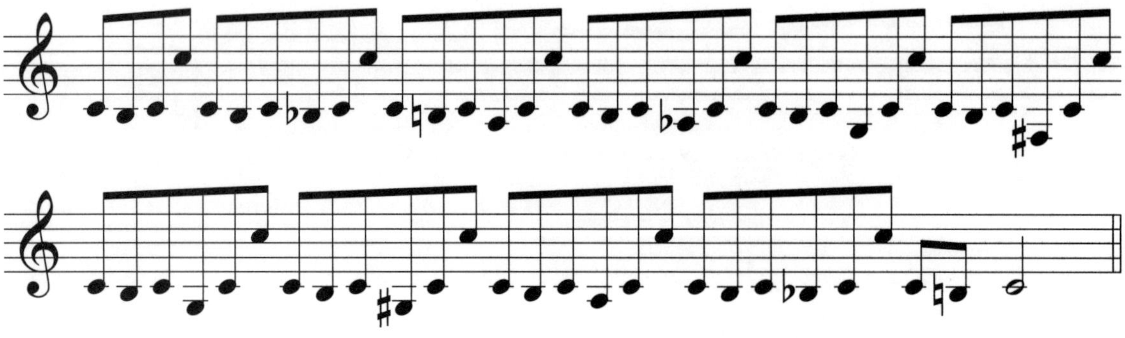

QUICK REGISTER CHANGES • THREE

Leave the mouthpiece on throughout. Breathe through the nose, adding as many beats rest as necessary. Reset for each tempo change.

Three Slur throughout

Four Slur throughout

THREE • QUICK REGISTER CHANGES

Leave the mouthpiece on throughout. Breathe through the nose, adding as many beats rest as necessary. Reset for each tempo change.

Five Slur throughout

Six Slur throughout

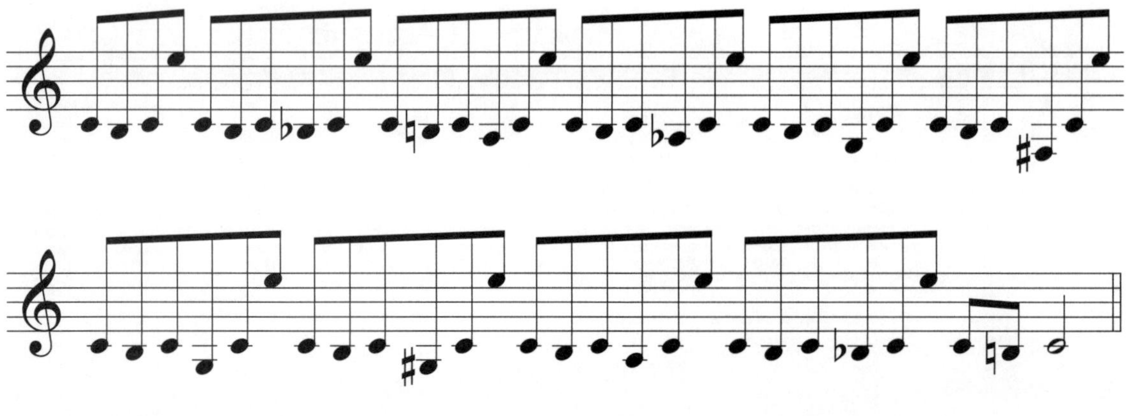

When the first part of this exercise can be played comfortably, add the coda.

Leave the mouthpiece on throughout. Breathe through the nose, adding as many beats rest as necessary. Reset for each tempo change.

Seven Slur throughout

THREE • QUICK REGISTER CHANGES

Breathe through the nose, adding as many beats rest as necessary. Reset for each tempo change.

Eight Slur throughout

Nine Slur throughout

QUICK REGISTER CHANGES • THREE

Breathe through the nose, adding as many beats rest as necessary. Reset for each tempo change.

Ten Slur throughout

THREE • QUICK REGISTER CHANGES

Eleven Slur throughout

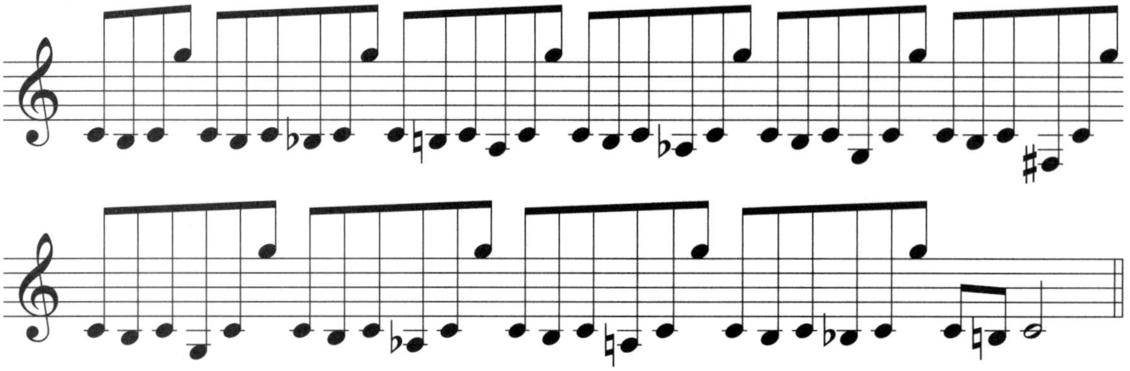

Twelve Slur throughout

QUICK REGISTER CHANGES • THREE

Maintain a consistent airstream through the initial chromatic figure and the progessively widening intervals.

One As fast as possible.

These exercises should also be played with this tongue/slur pattern:

Two

Three

Four

Five

FOUR • QUICK REGISTER CHANGES

FOUR • TARGET PRACTICE

When first doing these exercises, play a glissando between registers as in the following:

The glissando teaches the body to feel the distance between registers accurately. Once the correct movements are established, the glisses can be removed and the slurs played cleanly.

Transpose each line to G♯, A, B♭, B and C before moving on to the next line. Reset between each transposition.

One

Two

Three

Four Slur throughout

Five Slur throughout

Six Slur throughout

Seven Slur throughout

Eight Slur throughout

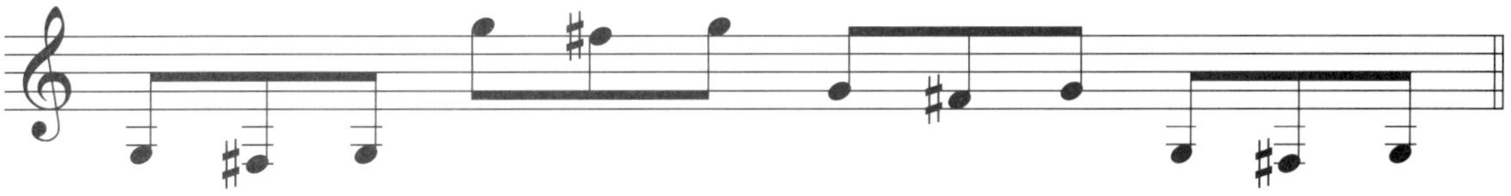

FOUR • QUICK REGISTER CHANGES

Nine Slur throughout

Ten Slur throughout

Eleven Slur throughout

Twelve Slur throughout

Thirteen Slur throughout

FIVE • OCTAVE DISPLACEMENT

Octave displacement is a common technique used to create the angular melodic lines often found in contemporary music. However, considerable skill is neeeded in order to make it a part of your improvisational repertoire. To develop this skill, begin with an exercise that is tonal and easily heard, such as the one below. Once you have developed the ability to comfortably play Exercises One through Three, atonal exercises such as those on pages 128 and 129 will be easier to execute.

Exercises One through Three are based on the following line. The first four pitches are then displaced whenever they occur—first up, then down.

One

Two

Three

ETUDE SEVEN

mp
mf
f
ff

FIVE • QUICK REGISTER CHANGES

One device used to organize modern improvisation is the 12 tone row. When using this material, octave displacement is often employed to add variety and interest. Unlike the exercises on pages 122 through 125, octave displacement of atonal material presents challenges because of the difficulty in anticipating the sound of the next pitch.

When improvising, not knowing the sound of the next pitch can result in the embouchure using extraneous motion to coordinate itself, and often missing the pitch entirely. For this reason, it is essential to learn to sing the tone rows and as many of the exercises as your vocal range allows.

These exercises use octave displacement of the following 12 tone row. Practice very slowly at first, and gradually work towards playing the exercises as fast as possible.

These first two exercises displace every other note up an octave. Use a variety of tongue/slur patterns. In general, try slurring any interval of a fifth or less. This would mean that the second line would contain no slurs at all. You can and should try to slur an occasional wide interval such as a seventh or ninth.

One

Two

Remember to keep a steady airstream throughout.

This exercise displaces the first note of alternating groups of two and three notes. Another interesting possibility would be to arrange the octave displacement in groups of two, two and three notes.

Three

Practice octave displacement, both up and down, with the following tone rows. Begin by displacing every other note, then every third note, etc. Use combinations of two- and three-note groups as in Exercise Three above.

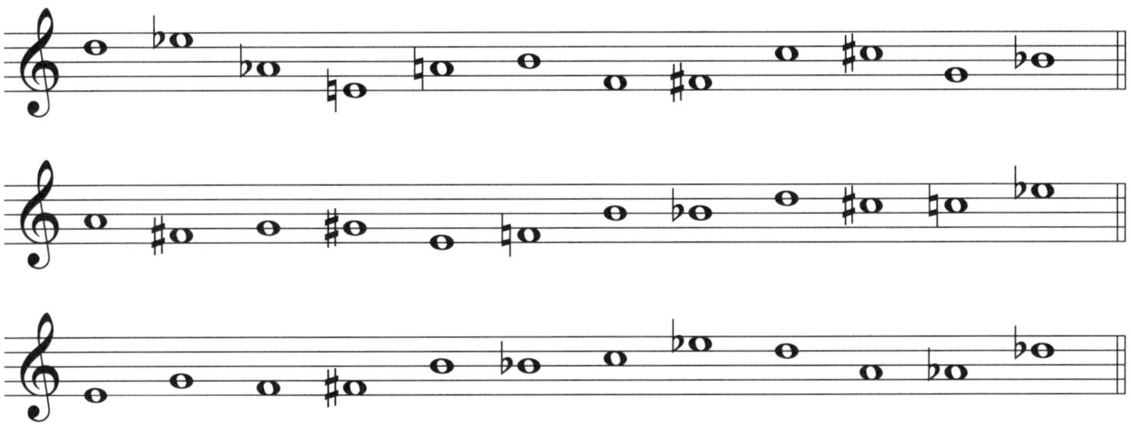

ETUDE EIGHT

f
ff
p

ETUDE • QUICK REGISTER CHANGES

ETUDE NINE

QUICK REGISTER CHANGES • ETUDE

ETUDE TEN

CD CONTENTS

INTRODUCTION

TRACK		
1	THOUGHTS ON PRACTICING	
2	HOW TO USE THIS BOOK	
3	WHEN TO MOVE ON	
4	HOW TO APPLY CALISTHENICS TO MUSIC	

PRELIMINARY STUDIES

5	THE LIP BEND	

FLEXIBILITY

6	BASIC FLEXIBILITY	Exercises 3 and 4, page 19
7		Exercise 11, page 23
8	FLEXANDO	Exercise 3, page 26
9	ADVANCED FLEXIBILITY	Exercises 8 and 9, page 34
10		Exercises 1 and 2, pages 36, 37
11	INTERVAL STUDIES	Exercise 1, page 44
12	ETUDE # 1: Discussion/alternate fingerings	page 49

ARTICULATION

13	SLURRING/TONGUING	Exercise 1, pages 54-55
14	DEVELOPED SCALE	Exercise 2, pages 62-63
15	ARPEGGIOS/DIRECTION CHANGES	Exercise 1, page 74 Exercises 1 and 5, page 81

PEDAL TONES

16	DISCUSSION/DEMONSTRATION	pages 85, 87-88

QUICK REGISTER CHANGES

17	CONSISTENT INTERVALS	Exercises 3 and 4, page 91
18		Exercises 2 and 3, page 94
19	SPIDERS	Exercise 1, page 98
20	CHROMATIC DISPLACEMENT	Exercise 3, page 107
21	TARGET PRACTICE	pages 118-119
22	OCTAVE DISPLACEMENT	pages 122-123
23	ETUDE #7, Discussion	pages 126-127
24	TWELVE TONE STUDIES: Discussion	pages 128-131